THE
SUPREMES'
GREATEST
HITS

REVISED & UPDATED EDITION

THE SUPREMES' GREATEST HITS

REVISED & UPDATED EDITION

THE 37 SUPREME COURT CASES
THAT MOST DIRECTLY AFFECT YOUR LIFE

Michael G. Trachtman

STERLING

New York / London
www.sterlingpublishing.com

STERLING and the distinctive Sterling logo are registered trademarks of
Sterling Publishing Co., Inc.

Frontispiece: U.S. Supreme Court Building, ca. 1943.

Library of Congress Cataloging-in-Publication Data
Trachtman, Michael G.
The Supremes' greatest hits : the 37 Supreme Court cases that most directly
affect your life / Michael G. Trachtman. — Rev. & updated ed.
p. cm.
Includes bibliographical references and index.
ISBN 978-1-4027-6826-2 (hc-trade cloth : alk. paper) 1. United States. Supreme Court.
2. Judicial review—United States--Cases. 3. Constitutional law—United States—Cases.
4. Law—United States—Popular works. I. Title.
KF8742.T73 2009
347.73'260264—dc22   2009008423

1   3   5   7   9   10   8   6   4   2

Published by Sterling Publishing Co., Inc.
387 Park Avenue South, New York, NY 10016

For picture credits please see page 243

Distributed in Canada by Sterling Publishing
c/o Canadian Manda Group, 165 Dufferin Street
Toronto, Ontario, Canada M6K 3H6
Distributed in the United Kingdom by GMC Distribution Services
Castle Place, 166 High Street, Lewes, East Sussex, England BN7 1XU
Distributed in Australia by Capricorn Link (Australia) Pty. Ltd.
P.O. Box 704, Windsor, NSW 2756, Australia

Book design and layout: JAM design

Sterling ISBN 978-1-4027-6826-2

For information about custom editions, special sales, premium and
corporate purchases, please contact Sterling Special Sales
Department at 800-805-5489 or specialsales@sterlingpublishing.com.

CONTENTS

ACKNOWLEDGMENTS

It was John Boswell's idea that this book should be written, and that I should be the one to write it. I am incredibly grateful for his creativity and generosity, and for the help he has freely given me in my effort to fulfill his vision.

Lawyers sometimes forget how to write and think like non-lawyers. My wife, Jennie, provided invaluable simultaneous translation services as I struggled to overcome those disabilities. Many apologies to her and my son, Ben, for the attention paid to this manuscript at their expense, and many more thanks for their understanding and encouragement.

"A GOVERNMENT OF LAWS, NOT MEN"

High school civics students are taught that our system of government is comprised of three branches: the legislature makes the laws; the executive enforces the laws; and the courts interpret the laws. As for the Supreme Court, they know that it is the highest court in the land—the final word on legal disputes.

So far as it goes, all of this is true. But to describe the Supreme Court in this way is to describe champagne as grape juice, or the Grand Canyon as a river valley—accurate to a point, but so shallow and incomplete as to be grotesquely misleading. Over 175 years ago, Alexis de Tocqueville, the celebrated French political observer, studied the Supreme Court and concluded, "A more imposing judicial power was never constituted by any people." The same holds true today.

The Ultimate Check and Balance: "Judicial Review"

Like the highest courts of other democracies, the Supreme Court has the authority to decide, once and for all, what important laws really mean when applied to the real-life situations that arise after the laws are enacted. Does the Civil Rights Act of 1964 protect women against sexual harassment? Does the Americans with Disabilities Act cover people with certain heart conditions? Various lower courts disagreed. The Supreme Court interpreted the wording and intent of the statutes and made a ruling. End of controversy.

But the most momentous role the Supreme Court plays in our society extends well beyond interpreting statutes: the Supreme Court serves as the ultimate interpreter and protector of our most fundamental rights—the rights set forth in the Constitution. Most historians agree that the American Constitution is the oldest national constitution still in effect, and it has stood the test of time for a reason. The framers of the Constitution drafted a document that was definitive in many respects, but also sufficiently vague so that it could be applied to unimaginable, changing circumstances. The framers of the Constitution knew things would change—as, of course, they did: no one could have anticipated the industrial revolution, or the aftermath of slavery, or World War II, or the Internet. They needed a mechanism to breathe continuing life into the Constitution. They needed, and therefore created, the Supreme Court.

The Supreme Court keeps the Constitution alive in two related ways. First, in the same way it interprets statutes, it interprets the Constitution. Does the First Amendment right of free speech allow you to burn the flag as a political statement? Does the Constitution's "Commerce Clause" allow Congress to outlaw racial discrimination, or Internet pornography? Supreme Court justices decide these issues, and the myriad of other questions that define our rights and lifestyles, through a process that is both rooted in historical precedent and at the same time highly intuitive and dependent on individual value judgments and philosophies. Through it all, the goal is to somehow determine what a group of eighteenth-century scholars, farmers, businessmen, soldiers, and politicians really meant by the words they wrote, and what they would have done if faced with a twenty-first century they could not have hoped to envision.

The second way the Supreme Court empowers the Constitution is what stupefied Tocqueville and so many others who have studied our democracy: the Supreme Court has the authority to decide that any act of a government official, and any law passed by a government body, violates the Constitution and is therefore invalid and of no effect. This power, termed the power of "judicial review," is virtually limitless. It encompasses the right to void the decisions of township officials, mayors, governors, and the president of the United States. It includes the right to strike from the books any township ordinance, state law, or Act of Congress. Supreme Court justices are appointed for life and, therefore, do not have to worry about making the popular decision, as opposed to the right decision. They can just say no.

This is a remarkable aspect of the American way of life. Through its proper exercise, the Supreme Court can ensure that it is the Constitution— not the people who happen to populate the Congress or the White House or the local city hall at any given time—that defines the extent to which our property and liberty can be compromised by our government.

This ultimate check and balance makes us what billions of people in the world strive to be—what John Adams first called a "government of laws, not men."

The Supreme Court has not been shy about using its authority. At times, the Supreme Court justices have made decisions that were welcomed when they were handed down, but are now seen as horrifically wrong, even repugnant. At other times, they have made decisions that were reviled, but are now seen as bastions of freedom and wisdom. Either way, it is difficult to overstate the influence the Supreme Court wields. The Supreme Court desegregated American schools. The Supreme Court allowed the internment of Japanese-Americans during World War II. The Supreme Court decided who you may, and may not, refuse to serve or hire in your restaurant or accounting firm. The Supreme Court decided what your rights will be if your employer sexually harasses you. The Supreme Court decreed and defined the right to an abortion. The Supreme Court decided how the forty-third president of the United States would be elected. The Supreme Court determined when your town council may appropriate your backyard and make it a parking lot for a shopping mall.

And it will be the Supreme Court that will resolve the hot-button issues of the twenty-first century. Will your school board be permitted to require your child to study "intelligent design" over your objection? To what extent will the federal government be permitted to monitor your e-mails and bank accounts in the name of national security? How far can we go in the effort to effectively limit the influence of corporate money in American elections? How will we deal with the myriad of issues, some known and many yet to be discovered, that the Internet and related technologies will present?

There is no appeal from a Supreme Court decision. It speaks last.

It is not surprising that the appointment of a Supreme Court justice stirs passions, argument, and multimillion-dollar lobbying efforts—few persons in our society have more power to define how we live.

What Exactly *Is* the Constitution?

During the Revolutionary War, the colonies were bound together through the Articles of Confederation, which created a very loose central government comprised only of Congress. Because there was no national president or judiciary, Congress had no way to enforce what it decreed, and it was left to the various states to comply on, essentially. a voluntary basis. The states were often less than cooperative, and many sought to compete, rather than cooperate, with each other. It was obvious that the colonies would never become a "nation" under the Articles, and this reality created the impetus for the Constitutional Convention in Philadelphia, at which the Constitution was drafted in 1787. The Constitution then had to be ratified by each of the states, a process that took two years of contentious proceedings, after which the Constitution became effective in 1789.

The Constitution is, by its own words, the "supreme law of the land." Most of the Constitution deals with the creation of a federal government—establishing the three branches; defining their powers; and, very important to the framers, limiting their powers. Several of the cases discussed later focus on the national crises that have accompanied the battles among the branches of government, and the battles among the federal government and the states over the limits of their respective spheres of authority. It is always left to the Supreme Court to interpret the Constitution and resolve these potential fractures in the system—as, for example, when Truman took it upon himself to seize the steel industry during the Korean War, or when Nixon refused to turn over his tapes to Congress in the Watergate scandal.

The Bill of Rights

The Bill of Rights is comprised of the first ten amendments to the Constitution. The fear among many of the Founding Fathers and many of the states was that the central government created by the Constitution could become tyrannical if the people were not guaranteed certain basic rights. Spurred by those concerns, within a few years after the Constitution was adopted, the Bill of Rights, encompassing many of our most fundamental bedrock freedoms, was finalized and ratified by the states. As Justice Robert H. Jackson once explained it, "The very purpose of a Bill of Rights was to withdraw certain subjects from the vicissitudes of political controversy, to place them beyond the reach of majorities and officials and to establish them as legal principles to be applied by the courts."

The essence of the Bill of Rights is set forth below.

FIRST AMENDMENT: This amendment prohibits the government from making any laws "respecting an establishment of
religion," or prohibiting "the free exercise" of religion, or
"abridging the freedom of speech." The First Amendment
also protects the right of the people to assemble and petition
the government for redress of grievances.

SECOND AMENDMENT: This amendment includes the often-
quoted "right of the people to keep and bear arms."

THIRD AMENDMENT: This amendment, a reaction to the way in
which the British treated the colonists, provides that no sol-
dier shall be quartered in any house without the consent of
the owner.

FOURTH AMENDMENT: This amendment protects the people
against "unreasonable searches and seizures" by the government and requires that warrants be issued only on probable
cause, and with specificity.

FIFTH AMENDMENT: This amendment provides a multitude of
rights. It defines how certain indictments must issue. It protects people against "double jeopardy" (that is, being tried
twice for the same crime). It provides the right against self-
incrimination. It provides that persons may not be "deprived
of life, liberty, or property, without due process of law." And it
provides that private property may be taken by the government
for public use, but that just compensation must be paid.

SIXTH AMENDMENT: This amendment provides criminal defendants with the right to a speedy and public trial by an impartial jury. It also provides a defendant with the right to be

informed of the charges made, to confront the witnesses against him, to subpoena his own witnesses, and to have the assistance of counsel.

SEVENTH AMENDMENT: This amendment provides for the right to a jury trial in certain civil cases.

EIGHTH AMENDMENT: This amendment prohibits "cruel and unusual punishment" and forbids excessive bail and excessive fines.

NINTH AMENDMENT: This amendment clarifies that although the Constitution provides certain rights to the people, it is not to be interpreted as diminishing all of the other rights the people have under the law—in other words, the Constitution is not the only source of the people's rights.

TENTH AMENDMENT: This amendment provides that all rights not delegated by the Constitution to the federal government are to be retained by the states or the people.

A great many Supreme Court cases focus on the effort to define and protect the rights of Americans as set forth in the Bill of Rights—and what to do when those rights conflict with one another. Several of those cases are discussed in the chapters that follow.

The Fourteenth Amendment

The Fourteenth Amendment to the Constitution was passed in 1868. It includes various sections, but the most renowned section includes the provisions known as the "Due Process Clause" and the "Equal Protection Clause," which guarantee basic freedoms that, like the Bill of

Rights, have been continuing focal points for the Supreme Court: "No State shall make or enforce any law which shall abridge the privileges or immunities of citizens of the United States; nor shall any State deprive any person of life, liberty, or property, without due process of law; nor deny to any person within its jurisdiction the equal protection of the laws."

The specific wording of the Bill of Rights prohibited the *federal* government, but not the *state* governments, from compromising fundamental freedoms. The Fourteenth Amendment was enacted in the wake of the Emancipation Proclamation in order to make it clear that, at the very least, the states owed constitutional duties of due process and equal protection to all persons. Ultimately, the Fourteenth Amendment was interpreted by the Supreme Court to require that the states also respect the core provisions of the Bill of Rights, such as free speech, the free exercise of religion, the right to counsel, and so on.

Particularly in the twentieth century, the Supreme Court has addressed numerous issues arising from the reluctance of some states to comply with notions of due process and equal protection and to fairly apply the Bill of Rights. This has led to colossal societal changes, such as desegregation, restrictions on the role of religion in schools and government, and the rights of the accused. Some of the most important of these cases are explained in the chapters that follow.

How the Supreme Court Works

The cases in this book illuminate how the Supreme Court has interpreted the Constitution and used its power of judicial review to define, and redefine, our way of life. To better understand how these cases came to be decided, it helps to understand what the Supreme Court is and how it goes about its business.

The Supreme Court is comprised of a chief justice and eight associate justices, all of whom are nominated by the president and confirmed with the "advice and consent" of the Senate. The senatorial confirmation process entails a detailed investigation, a lengthy Judiciary Committee hearing, and a full Senate vote. Particularly in the last twenty years, Senate confirmation has become a harrowing experience, drawing extensive television coverage and well-funded lobbying efforts reinforced by major media campaigns.

Presidents typically nominate someone they believe will share their political and judicial philosophies, but the history of the Supreme Court is replete with justices who were supposed to be of one stripe, and turned out to be much different. A lifetime appointment to a position with the power to change fundamental rights and national policies, free from direct political pressures, can easily change one's perspective and ideology.

President Eisenhower, for instance, appointed Chief Justice Earl Warren, believing that he would be a conservative jurist. Warren turned out to be one of the most liberal and activist chief justices in history, prompting Eisenhower to call the appointment "the biggest damn-fool mistake I ever made." When Justice David Souter was nominated in 1990, the National Organization of Women, believing he would seek to overturn *Roe v. Wade*, distributed flyers blaring "Stop Souter or Women Will Die." After he was confirmed, Justice Souter helped write the opinion reaffirming the continuing validity of *Roe v. Wade*.

In rare instances, such as boundary line disputes between states, the litigants have a right to bring their claim directly to the Supreme Court. Otherwise, the Supreme Court gets to choose the cases it hears. After a case has been decided by a lower state or federal court, a litigant has the right to file a petition with the Supreme Court seeking a "writ of certiorari," the technical term for the writ the Supreme Court issues when it agrees to hear and decide an appeal.

Typically, the Court will consider something in the neighborhood of seven thousand such petitions a year. In the selection process, the justices look for cases of constitutional significance and other matters of national importance. After an initial screening process that eliminates most of the petitions, the justices meet to consider the remaining petitions on Wednesdays and Fridays in a secure conference room, in which no outsiders are allowed. The justices study the petitions well in advance of this conference, and, after the chief justice opens the discussion by summarizing each case, each justice then speaks, in order of seniority. The most junior justice has the task of guarding the door: if reference material or anything else is needed, the junior justice notifies an attendant stationed outside of the conference room, and then, outside the door, receives whatever was requested. No one enters the room.

It takes a vote of four justices to "grant cert," as it is colloquially called. If "cert" is not granted, the decision of the lower court remains undisturbed. From the thousands of petitions for certiorari it receives each year, in the 1980s the Court accepted approximately 150 cases per year on which it rendered written decisions. That number dropped to about 80 cases per year under Chief Justice Rehnquist. Recently appointed Chief Justice Roberts has indicated a desire to increase that number.

Each Supreme Court term begins on the first Monday in October. Well before each Court session, the lawyers representing the parties submit detailed briefs, which the justices carefully study. During Court sessions, which are open to the public, the lawyers present oral arguments to the justices. Frequently, individual justices will interrupt and ask the lawyers difficult and pointed questions, sometimes for the purpose of honestly exploring the merits of an issue, sometimes for the purpose of reinforcing a favored position or tearing down a disfavored position in the hope of building support among the other justices.

After oral arguments, a conference is scheduled, at which the justices discuss and vote on how they believe a case should be decided, at least at that point. If the chief justice is in the majority, he assigns either himself or another justice to write the majority opinion; if not, the senior justice who is in the majority makes that assignment. Other justices may write their own concurring or dissenting opinions. The opinions are then circulated among the justices in the effort to build as much consensus as possible. Debates continue, and opinions are revised, as the justices continue to exchange views among themselves.

Ultimately, each justice decides whether he or she will subscribe to the majority opinion. A justice who votes with the majority may also write a concurring opinion, explaining his or her own views. Justices who do not subscribe to the majority view may write dissenting opinions to explain the bases for their position. Most cases are decided clearly and decisively, but approximately twenty percent of the cases carry only a 5–4 majority, and some cases are so difficult and contentious that they generate numerous opinions, none of which garners the support of a majority.

What if the Supreme Court Issued an Order . . . and No One Listened?

It is frequently said that the Supreme Court has no army—a pithy way to make the point that the Supreme Court has no way to independently enforce its rulings. Consequently, the Court depends on the will of the other branches of government, usually the president, to carry out its decisions, as when troops were called in to enforce school desegregation after *Brown v. Board of Education*.

We take it for granted that what the Supreme Court says, goes. Still, there are nightmare scenarios that are difficult to contemplate. As many of the cases in the following chapters demonstrate, sometimes the Supreme Court has to take on the president head-on, and sometimes a true reading of the Constitution requires the Court to take an extremely unpopular position. If a president openly defied a Supreme Court order, what then? If the president were backed by the polls, would Congress have the political will to pursue impeachment in order to protect the Constitution? How would that battle play out?

These are the kinds of upheavals that plague countries without engrained constitutional traditions, where might makes right. At least for now, our tradition and culture make these scenarios unlikely; respect for the highest court's interpretation of the Constitution is, after all, at the root of what defines "a government of laws, not men."

But whether this remains the case will depend on whether the justices are viewed, beyond rational doubt, as serving only the Constitution, and not their own political agendas or social or religious philosophies. If the good faith of those who make up the Supreme Court ever comes into serious question, the moral authority of the Court—which is, really, the only authority the Court ultimately has—will evaporate, with disastrous results.

The following chapters explain some of the Supreme Court decisions that have had the greatest impact on our history and character, and that most affect the everyday lives of Americans. The intention is to enable the reader to appreciate the mammoth difficulty and consequence of the issues the Supreme Court has had to wrestle with, and to allow the reader to reach an informed judgment on whether the Supreme Court has earned its moral authority.

Some of these decisions resonate from the past; others deal exclusively with twenty-first-century issues; all of them help define who we are and where we are going. They illuminate the tensions between individual liberty and the interests of society, the challenge of balancing majority rule with minority rights, the difficulties of applying old laws to new technologies and changing cultures, and the need to address crises in the short term while preserving fundamental rights in the long term. Like it or not, each of us, and our children who come after us, will be affected, even transformed, by what these decisions say.

CHAPTER 1

HOW THE SUPREME COURT BECAME SUPREME

"We are not final because we are infallible, but
we are infallible only because we are final."

— JUSTICE ROBERT H. JACKSON

The Supreme Court was not always so supreme. It took the
Supreme Court's own decision to create this prerogative—in
effect, the Supreme Court created its own preeminence.

This seminal decision was rendered in the 1803 case of *Marbury v.
Madison*, which gave the Supreme Court the right of "judicial review"—
the power, mentioned previously, to determine what is and is not constitutional, and the coordinate right to void governmental actions and
laws if they violate the Constitution. This power to ensure compliance
with the Constitution not only defined the landscape of our own
democracy, it served as a model for constitutional democracies
throughout the world.

As would ultimately be seen, however, the power to decide takes with
it the power to decide wrongly. And the impact of a wrong decision by
the Supreme Court can change the face of society, reverberating for
decades, even centuries.

Portraits of influential chief justices of the Supreme Court are depicted in a c. 1894 print. Counter-
clockwise from top left: John Jay, John Rutledge, Oliver Ellsworth, John Marshall, Roger Brook
Taney, Salmon Portland Chase, Morrison R. Waite, and Melville W. Fuller.

1. Marbury v. Madison

Chief Justice Marshall 1803

Marbury v. Madison arose from the uncertainties that characterized the first years after the Constitution was ratified—no one could be sure of exactly what the Constitution would come to mean in practice, and the branches of government openly jockeyed for position. As for the Supreme Court, the framers had not specifically delineated how much influence it should have, and this issue provoked much debate and disagreement. Many felt that the most the Supreme Court could do was interpret laws, not overrule them. Indeed, in the early days of our country, the Supreme Court did not even have its own building (Congress graciously allowed it to conduct business in an unused committee room in the basement of the Capitol), and its role as an equal—let alone preeminent—branch of government was anything but plain.

The seeds of change, however, were planted in 1800, when Republican Thomas Jefferson defeated incumbent Federalist John Adams in a bitterly contested election. Just before he left office, Adams attempted to entrench Federalist judges in the judiciary by appointing sixteen new circuit judges and forty-two new justices of the peace. However, due to a last-minute administrative mix-up as Adams left and Jefferson arrived, one of the appointees, Marbury, did not receive his written commission appointing him as a justice of the peace, even though it had been signed by then-president Adams and confirmed by the Senate.

Jefferson and the Republicans bore much hostility toward the Federalists; and Jefferson, flexing his political muscles and testing the boundaries of presidential power, refused to issue the commission to Marbury. In effect, Jefferson declared that he had the power to do what he pleased, and he dared Marbury to do something about it.

David Versus Goliath: Marbury Strikes Back

Marbury was incensed, and he turned to the courts for help. He sued the iconic James Madison, Jefferson's secretary of state (the government official in technical possession of the commission), seeking an order requiring that the commission be delivered to him. Jefferson was not pleased.

Marbury filed his lawsuit against Madison directly in the Supreme Court. Normally, a lawsuit would have to wend its way through the lower courts before the Supreme Court would even think about considering it, but Congress had passed a statute, the Judiciary Act of 1789, that allowed suits like the one brought by Marbury to bypass the lower courts and proceed in this rather unusual way.

Chief Justice Marshall felt that Marbury had been wronged by Jefferson, but he also felt that the Judiciary Act of 1789 violated the Constitution. Marshall's view was that the Constitution did not permit lawsuits like Marbury's to be filed in the Supreme Court, and he believed that Congress had overstepped its authority by enacting a statute that contradicted the Constitution's plain language.

Marshall's Masterstroke

Marbury's lawsuit presented on a silver platter the issue that Chief Justice Marshall longed to decide: whether the judiciary had the power to declare unconstitutional and therefore invalidate a law, in this case the Judiciary Act of 1789, that had been passed by a duly elected legislature and signed by a duly elected president, each of which comprises an equal branch of government. How could the three branches of government be equal if, in fact, one could effectively negate the actions of the other? Or, as Marshall put it through superlative understatement, "The question, whether an act, repugnant to the constitution, can become the law of the land, is a question deeply interesting to the United States."

At the same time, Marshall realized that he was not merely deciding an important legal issue—he was defining the shape of the American system of government for succeeding generations. He knew that if he found in favor of Marbury and ordered Jefferson to issue the writ, Jefferson would likely ignore the order. He also knew that if he denied Marbury's claim, it would appear that the Court had kowtowed to the president. Either way, Marshall knew that, depending on what he did, the Court could be forever relegated to second-class status. And, knowing his legacy rested in the balance, Marshall was not about to allow that to happen.

Marshall, as adept at politics as he was at law, crafted a solution that, to this day, is recognized as a consummate judicial tour de force.

Initially, Marshall declared that Marbury should have received his commission, chastising Jefferson and avoiding the appearance of judicial subservience.

Marshall then ruled unconstitutional the act of Congress, the Judiciary Act of 1789, that gave the Supreme Court the power to hear Marbury's case and reverse what Jefferson had done. Bad news for Marbury; but in so doing, Marshall dodged a confrontation with Jefferson and simultaneously gave himself the opportunity to establish, once and for all, the right of the Supreme Court to void any law that the Supreme Court deemed, in its sole judgment, to violate the Constitution. Marshall capitalized on that opportunity, using logic and language that has resonated throughout our history.

Marshall wrote that the American people had a right to "establish, for their future government, such principles as, in their opinion, shall most conduce to their own happiness," and had done so in the form of a written Constitution. The Constitution represents the "original and supreme will" of the people and "is the basis on which the whole American fabric has been erected." From this, Marshall's ultimate conclusion, on which so much of America as it exists today is founded, logically followed:

"Certainly all those who have framed written constitutions contemplate them as forming the fundamental and paramount law of the nation, and consequently the theory of every such government must be that an act of the legislature repugnant to the constitution is void."

The Legacy of *Marbury v. Madison*

Consider where we might be had Chief Justice Marshall not taken this judicial leap of faith. Without *Marbury v. Madison* and the principles it entrenched, Congress, or a state legislature, or a local borough council would only be restrained by the fear of losing the next election. So long as the majority of voters remained either in favor of or apathetic about what government did, government officials could pass laws designed to eliminate free speech among their critics, arbitrarily restrict the use of private property, favor their race or religion over others, gerrymander election districts to effectively fix elections, and so on. In essence, they could do whatever they wanted, for so long as they could successfully manipulate the political process and stay in office.

But after *Marbury v. Madison* the rule book changed, and the players had to change along with it: now, government officials know that at any time, a single citizen armed with a creative lawyer can invoke the power of the judiciary to measure their laws and decisions against constitutional standards. Each citizen, through this right to invoke the overriding authority of the Constitution, can play a direct role in controlling government, instead of government controlling each citizen. *Marbury v. Madison* gave us the opportunity to remain the government of laws, not men, that is a prime hallmark of our greatness as a nation.

To this day, virtually all constitutional law courses begin with *Marbury v. Madison*, and constitutional democracies throughout the world revere the decision as the wellspring of the checks and balances that make a true and lasting democracy feasible.

2. Dred Scott v. Sandford

Did the Supreme Court Trigger the Civil War? 1857

The infamous *Dred Scott v. Sandford* decision was the first case since *Marbury v. Madison*, decided more than fifty years earlier, in which the Supreme Court used the power of judicial review to declare an act of Congress unconstitutional. It had all the elements of a Hollywood thriller—human pathos, a burning national crisis, backroom deals, moral activists facing off against big business, ethical weakness at the highest levels of government, the rise of an unknown crusader into the pantheon of history. Everything, that is, except a happy ending. The *Dred Scott* case reinforced the role of the Supreme Court as the institution to which American society turns for the final and binding decisions on its most incendiary issues. It also serves as the exemplar of how much damage can be done when the power of judicial review goes awry.

At its core, in the *Dred Scott* decision the Supreme Court ruled that slaves and free blacks were *not* citizens worthy of constitutional protection, and could lawfully be claimed as property, even in states that had outlawed slavery. The decision placed a stamp of approval on slavery, put a match to an already-smoldering blood feud between North and South, and accelerated a chain of events that ultimately elected Lincoln and overwhelmed whatever opportunity there had been to avoid civil war.

This "self-inflicted wound" (as one future justice described the case) seriously diminished the prestige and power of the Court for at least a generation.

Dred Scott's Suit for Freedom

After the ratification of the Constitution (which purposely failed to confront the legalities of slavery), the bitter fight between pro-slavery and anti-slavery forces intensified. This eventually led, in 1820, to the Missouri Compromise: as part of the admission of Maine and Missouri as states, Congress provided that (with the exception of Missouri itself) slavery would be prohibited in the territories north of the line that formed Missouri's southern border.

Dred Scott was a Virginia slave who had been sold to an army physician, Dr. Emerson, who, sometime after 1820, took him north of the Missouri Compromise line (where slavery was unlawful), and then back to Missouri (where slavery was lawful). In prior cases, numerous courts had ruled—and it was generally accepted—that once a slave set foot on free soil, he was emancipated. In 1850, Scott, who had saved some money, tried to buy his freedom from Dr. Emerson's widow, who now owned Scott. Dr. Emerson's widow refused, and Scott brought suit in Missouri state court claiming that, having lived in the free territory, he was now a free man.

A jury found in Scott's favor, but the Missouri Supreme Court reversed, ruling that it was "a humiliating spectacle to see a court of a state confiscate the property of her own citizens by the command of a foreign law." In other words, Dred Scott was property, and a contrary law enacted by a Congress situated far away, in Washington, D.C., was a "foreign law" that need not be followed.

Dred Scott's attorney responded by dropping his claims in state court and filing a lawsuit in federal court. Scott's position was this: citizens can sue in federal court; Scott was a citizen by virtue of his journey to a free territory; and the Missouri Compromise, a federal law, should be enforced for his benefit.

Scott lost, and the Supreme Court accepted the appeal.

Scott's case crystallized the most combustible issues of the time. Is a freed black a "citizen" who is entitled to protection under the Constitution, or merely property to be bought and sold? Does the federal government have the constitutional power to tell the states what to do about slavery?

As the Supreme Court mulled over the issues, the country became embroiled in a hurricane of pro-slavery versus anti-slavery debate. As emotions rose, Stephen A. Douglas, a well-known Illinois senator and orator, introduced a bill in Congress that sought to invalidate the Missouri Compromise in Kansas and Nebraska so that those states could decide the slavery issue for themselves, free from federal interference. This further outraged the North, leading to the formation of a new party, the Republican Party, which passionately opposed the extension of slavery into the territories. Angry and concerned citizens in both the North and South gathered and argued on street corners and in town halls.

The Decision and Its Aftermath: North v. South

Chief Justice Roger Taney announced the Supreme Court's decision on March 6, 1857. Joined by six other justices, he wrote that blacks had been regarded as holding an inferior status when the Constitution was adopted, and were therefore not "citizens" entitled to sue in federal court. That ruling effectively put Dred Scott out of court, and there was no reason for the decision to go further. But Chief Justice Taney did not stop there.

Invoking the Court's judicial review powers, Chief Justice Taney went on to rule that Congress had exceeded its constitutional authority when it enacted the Missouri Compromise. As a result, Dred Scott could no longer argue that because he had been taken to a free territory he was therefore emancipated—the Missouri Compromise was invalid and without legal effect, and consequently the territory north of the Missouri Compromise line was no longer free. Moreover, said Chief Justice Taney, it would be unconstitutional to deem a slave a free man merely because the slave had been taken into free territory, since that would deprive the slave owner of his rightful property, the slave, without just compensation: the government could not take a man's farm or livestock without paying him, and neither could it take a man's slaves.

The upshot was that slaves were to remain slaves, and the federal government had been stripped of the authority to do much about it.

Even formerly apathetic Northerners took the decision as a virtual call to arms, swelling the ranks of the militant abolitionists. Horace Greeley, the famed journalist and politician, owned the most influential newspaper of the time, the *New York Tribune*, in which he wrote that the *Dred Scott* decision "is entitled to just so much moral weight as would be the judgment of a majority of those congregated in any Washington bar-room." At the same time, the South was empowered, and Southern politicians and newspapers trumpeted the decision as a validation of states' rights, in particular the right of any established or new state to decide whether slavery would be legal within its borders, no matter what the federal government said.

Cynics speculated that some of the Supreme Court justices had been influenced by politics. Before the decision was reached, President-elect Buchanan (who had won the November 1856 election, but was still awaiting his inauguration) made no secret of the fact that he opposed the Missouri Compromise and wanted it overturned. In recent years, historians have uncovered evidence of patently unethical communications in which Buchanan lobbied at least two of the justices to sign on to Taney's opinion.

Lincoln Enters the Controversy

A year after the *Dred Scott* decision was announced, Lincoln, then an unknown on the national stage, challenged Douglas, then a leading candidate for the Democratic presidential nomination, for Douglas's Illinois senate seat. Lincoln initiated his campaign with one of his most famous speeches. He stressed the injustice in the fact that, according to the *Dred Scott* decision, a slave could live in a free state and yet still be a slave. Said Lincoln: "A house divided against itself cannot stand. I believe this government cannot endure, permanently half slave and half free." In the months that followed, the candidates engaged in the famous Lincoln-Douglas debates, in which Lincoln repeatedly railed at the *Dred Scott* decision and all those who agreed that blacks were not entitled to protection under the precepts of the Declaration of Independence and the Constitution.

Douglas sought a middle ground, and in the process alienated both Northern and Southern voters. In the 1860 presidential campaign, Douglas got the Democratic nomination, but Southerners bolted from the party and nominated their own pro-slavery ticket. The Whigs also nominated their own ticket; and, riding the crest of the notoriety he obtained after *Dred Scott*, the Republican Party nominated Lincoln. This four-party election fractionalized the electorate—Lincoln received a minority of the popular vote, but won the electoral vote and, ironically, was sworn in as president by Chief Justice Taney himself in 1861.

Lincoln immediately faced Northerners who believed the *Dred Scott* decision would lead to future Supreme Court cases in which Northern states would be forbidden from banning slavery within their borders (Lincoln himself had fanned those flames in the Lincoln–Douglas debates). At the same time, he was confronted by Southerners who celebrated the prospect of slave auctions on the Boston Commons.

The rest, as the saying goes, is history.

Ultimately, the Fourteenth Amendment, adopted in 1868, provided that slaves were fully entitled to citizenship and constitutional protections, effectively overruling the *Dred Scott* decision and launching it into ignominy. That did little good in reality, however, as the so-called Black Codes of the Southern states imposed second-class status, and much worse, on Southern blacks until the federal government enacted and began to enforce, sometimes through military actions, meaningful civil rights legislation in the 1960s.

The *Dred Scott* case is, even today, cited as the poster child for those who decry "judicial activism." During his confirmation hearing, Chief Justice Roberts was asked if he agreed with a statement President Lincoln made in his first inaugural address. Lincoln said that if vital questions affecting the people were irrevocably decided by the Supreme Court (as opposed to the other branches of government), "the people will have ceased to be their own rulers." Chief Justice Roberts responded as follows:

> Well, President Lincoln, of course, was referring to one of the, perhaps the most, egregious examples of judicial activism in our history, the *Dred Scott* case. In which the court went far beyond what was necessary to decide the case, and really I think historians would say that the Supreme Court tried to put itself in the position of resolving the dispute about the extension of slavery and resolving it in a particular way that it thought was best for the nation. And we saw what disastrous consequences flowed from that.

As important as the *Dred Scott* decision is in the context of the Civil War and our larger history, there is another aspect to the case that makes it of foundational significance to our constitutional democracy: Lincoln abided by it. Lincoln excoriated the decision as both wrong and dangerous—and yet in the Lincoln-Douglas debates he argued that, nevertheless, it was a decision of the Supreme Court, and it must be respected until the Supreme Court says otherwise.

"We think its [the Supreme Court's] decisions on Constitutional questions, when fully settled, should control, not only the particular cases decided, but the general policy of the country, subject to be disturbed only by amendments of the Constitution as provided in that instrument itself," Lincoln said. And leaving no doubt as to his view on the supremacy of Supreme Court decisions, he then continued. "More than this would be revolution. But we think the *Dred Scott* decision is erroneous. We know the court that made it, has often over-ruled its own decisions, and we shall do what we can to have it to over-rule this. We offer no resistance to it."

This closed the loop on *Marbury v. Madison:* no matter how difficult the circumstances, no matter how entrenched the personal disagreements, the United States was to be a government of laws, not men.

As for Dred Scott himself, in 1857, Dr. Emerson's widow remarried. Her new husband opposed slavery, and she returned Scott to his former owners, the Blow family, who gave Scott and his family their freedom. The next year, Dred Scott died of tuberculosis. His gravesite in St. Louis County now bears the following marker:

DRED SCOTT BORN ABOUT 1799 DIED SEPT. 17, 1858. DRED SCOTT SUBJECT OF THE DECISION OF THE SUPREME COURT OF THE UNITED STATES IN 1857 WHICH DENIED CITIZEN-SHIP TO THE NEGRO, VOIDED THE MISSOURI COMPROMISE ACT, BECAME ONE OF THE EVENTS THAT RESULTED IN THE CIVIL WAR.

CHAPTER 2

ONE NATION UNDER GOD? MATTERS OF CHURCH AND STATE

"A union of government and religion tends to destroy government and degrade religion."

—JUSTICE HUGO L. BLACK

The phrase "separation of church and state" is engrained in the American vernacular—but, contrary to the common mythology, the phrase does not appear in the Constitution. Jefferson lobbied for, as he put it, "a wall of separation between church and state," but other Founding Fathers sought no more than a constitutional provision forbidding the government from enshrining a national religion. They wanted religious freedom, and feared the religious persecution that would result if government were permitted to endorse one religion over another.

When all was said and done, the framers of the Constitution inserted into the First Amendment a provision known as the "Establishment Clause," which as now interpreted, effectively provides that government "shall make no law respecting an establishment of religion."

The disagreement over what those words mean has spurred an ongoing constitutional holy war in which the hostilities continue, while the battlegrounds change.

In this 1891 Thomas Nast cartoon from *Harper's Weekly*, a woman symbolizing Justice stands at the door of a building labeled "State," as soldiers block the steps to members of different religions.

3. Engel v. Vitale

The School Prayer Case:
Religion in the Public Schools 1962

Legal scholars have debated the meaning of the Establishment Clause for decades. The words themselves do not reflect the adoption of Jefferson's point of view: there is no mandate that all religion be removed from the public arena. Still, at what point does the government's acceptance of or involvement in religion become "an establishment of religion"?

After a history of confusing and contradictory decisions, the Supreme Court began to clarify the practical meaning and impact of the Establishment Clause in the school prayer cases that captured the attention of the nation in the early 1960s.

Does School Prayer "Establish" Religion?

In many schools throughout the country, students were routinely required to begin the day with the recitation of a prayer. In New York, the state Board of Regents composed what they believed was a nondenominational prayer: "Almighty God, we acknowledge our dependence upon Thee, and we beg Thy blessing upon us, our parents, our teachers and our Country." The Regents suggested, but did not mandate, that the prayer be recited by all students at the commencement of each school day.

Claiming that the Regents' actions violated the Establishment Clause, a group of parents filed a lawsuit, *Engel v. Vitale*, which worked its way through the court system and eventually was heard by the Supreme Court.

Facing extreme pressure on both sides of the issue, a clear majority of the Supreme Court agreed that the Regents had overstepped their constitutional boundaries. Justice Black, writing for the majority, put the issue into its historical context, recalling "that this very practice of establishing governmentally composed prayers for religious services was one of the reasons which caused many of our early colonists to leave England and seek religious freedom in America." Justice Black reasoned that a prayer is by its very nature religious, and that "we think that the constitutional prohibition against laws respecting an establishment of religion must at least mean that in this country, it is no part of the business of government to compose official prayers for any group of the American people to recite as a part of a religious program carried on by government."

New York (and the many other states that supported its position) argued that the prayer could not constitute the establishment of religion because it was voluntary, and did not reference any particular faith. Justice Black was unpersuaded. The prayer, he reasoned, promotes religion, and that is enough, even if it is not coercive. And the fact that the prayer referred to no particular religion is inconsequential, since it still promotes a family of religions—those that believe in "Almighty God."

The Court's ultimate ruling was plainly stated: "We think that by using its public school system to encourage recitation of the Regents' prayer, the State of New York has adopted a practice wholly inconsistent with the Establishment Clause."

The rationale of *Engel v. Vitale*, handed down in 1962, was expanded and clarified the next year in the case of *Abington Township School District v. Schempp*, which declared the practice of school-sponsored Bible reading and the recitation of the Lord's Prayer to be similarly unconstitutional. The *Schempp* case is doubly significant. In it, the Supreme Court also laid down what is known as the "secular purpose" and "primary effect" tests for Establishment Clause cases: if either the purpose or the effect of a law or government action is to advance or inhibit religion, the Establishment Clause is implicated. Using these criteria, as well as similar criteria that evolved in subsequent Establishment Clause cases, the Supreme Court has ruled unconstitutional all manner of school-sponsored or school-endorsed prayers at graduation ceremonies and other school events.

The "Religion-Free Zone" Myth

The *Engel and Schempp* cases were the subject of much protest, and in the process their true meaning has become substantially distorted.

Neither case, as is so often stated, takes God out of the schools, or mandates that schools be "religion-free zones." *Engel* and *Schempp* in no way restrict the teaching of religion as a subject of academic study, and they do not prohibit individual students from saying a prayer, distributing religious literature, talking to students about their religious beliefs, forming Bible-study groups, or wearing religious clothing, subject to the same rules of orderly conduct and school administration as other, nonreligious behavior. The Supreme Court placed its focus on the role of government in promoting religion, not the role of students in practicing religion.

Even so, disagreements over the meaning of the Establishment Clause continue to abound. Many citizens (including several Supreme Court justices) stress that the framers of the Constitution were men who held not only an abiding belief in God, but also a belief that the nation itself owed its existence and future to God. Therefore, they argue, while the framers did indeed fear the establishment of a "state religion," they could not have intended to invalidate prayers and ceremonies that do no more than pay respect to God.

Engel and *Schempp* have been settled law for over forty years, and barring a dramatic shift in the makeup of the Court it is unlikely they will be overturned. On the school front, the Establishment Clause battleground has shifted from school ceremonies to school curriculum. The next battery of Supreme Court decisions in this area will likely define the difference between that which constitutes the teaching of science, ethics, or philosophy and that which constitutes the promotion and sponsorship of religion.

4. Epperson v. Arkansas

The Scopes "Monkey Trial" Revisited: The Teaching of Evolution, Creationism, and "Intelligent Design" in Public Schools 1968

In the 1920s, fundamentalist religious groups lobbied public schools to prohibit the teaching of evolution, linking it with atheism. William Jennings Bryan, former secretary of state, three-time presidential candidate, famous orator, and staunch fundamentalist, personally championed this movement, labeling the teaching of evolution irrational and immoral. (As Bryan was fond of saying during his many orations, "It is better to trust in the Rock of Ages than to know the ages of rock.") Largely as a result of his efforts, in 1925 Tennessee passed a law, known as the Butler Act, which forbade the teaching in public schools of "any theory that denies the story of the Divine Creation of man as taught in the Bible, and to teach instead that man has descended from a lower order of animals."

The Scopes "Monkey Trial"

The ACLU immediately offered to defend anyone convicted under the Butler Act. Sensing an opportunity to bring publicity and commerce to their town, within a few months a group of businessmen in Dayton, Tennessee, convinced a local biology teacher, John Scopes, to admit that he taught evolution and to invite prosecution as a test case. The prosecutors obliged.

Bryan immediately accepted an invitation to assist the prosecution. In response, Clarence Darrow, a staunch agnostic and one of the most famous lawyers and social crusaders of his day, volunteered to help the defense. The famous Scopes "Monkey Trial" was on.

The trial was covered by more than a hundred newspaper reporters from all parts of the country, as well as reporters from Europe. Twenty-two telegraphers sent out 165,000 words a day, and a Chicago radio station broadcast the trial nationally—the first live radio coverage of a criminal trial. Two movie cameramen had their film flown out daily from a specially prepared airstrip.

The defense originally challenged the Butler Act on Establishment Clause grounds, but Darrow took control, launched a frontal assault on Bryan himself, and called Bryan as a witness in the effort to get him to admit that whatever moral and religious teachings the Bible might provide, it was not "science" and could not be taken literally. Darrow's cross-examination of Bryan became the stuff of legend. Darrow took Bryan through the story of Jonah, accounts of the earth standing still, the story of creation as set forth in Genesis, whether Eve was actually created from Adam's rib, and so on. The exchanges between the two were blistering. Bryan accused Darrow of having no purpose other than "to cast ridicule on everybody who believes in the Bible." Darrow responded, "We have the purpose of preventing bigots and ignoramuses from controlling the education of the United States." (The play and movie *Inherit the Wind* dramatizes the trial, and the Darrow–Bryan confrontation in particular, but does so with much poetic license.)

Darrow knew that he could not possibly obtain an acquittal in the Dayton trial court—it was never contested that Scopes violated the Butler Act. He also knew that a challenge to the constitutionality of the Butler Act would be better pursued before an appeals court. Rather than trying to win the case in Dayton, Darrow's intent was to ridicule Bryan's position and turn public opinion against statutes like the Butler Act, and by many accounts he plainly succeeded. H. L. Mencken, a famous journalist who actually helped fund the defense, wrote that Bryan was a "buffoon" and that his speeches were "theologic bilge," while characterizing the defense as "eloquent" and "magnificent." *Life* magazine awarded Bryan its "Brass Medal of the Fourth Class," writing that he had "successfully demonstrated by the alchemy of ignorance hot air may be transmuted into gold, and that the Bible is infallibly inspired except where it differs with him on the question of wine, women, and wealth."

Outfoxing Bryan, at the close of the trial Darrow literally told the judge to find Scopes guilty, and Darrow gave no final summation. Under Tennessee procedures, if Darrow gave no final summation, Bryan would be barred from making a final summation as well. Darrow knew that Bryan had been hungering to deliver a speech that Bryan later called "the mountain peak of my life's effort," a fire-and-brimstone, anti-evolution, fundamentalist oration for the assembled journalists and radio audience, and Darrow's tactic ended the trial before Bryan had his opportunity.

After nine minutes of deliberation, the jury found Scopes guilty, and the judge ordered him to pay a $100 fine (which Bryan offered to pay on Scopes's behalf). The defense appealed to the Tennessee Supreme Court. Among other arguments, the defense contended that the Butler Act violated the Establishment Clause, and was therefore unconstitutional. The Tennessee Supreme Court refused to so rule—but found an "out" and reversed the conviction anyway, ruling that under Tennessee law, the jury, not the judge, was to have decided the amount of the fine.

Having had enough, the prosecution never sought a retrial. The "Monkey Trial" remained part of American history and legend, but had no significant impact on American law for more than forty years. In the meantime, the anti-evolutionists vigorously continued their efforts, and laws similar to the Butler Act were enacted in Mississippi and Arkansas. The ACLU was unable to find another teacher willing to go through what Scopes had endured, and it was not until the 1960s, spurred by the

Supreme Court's Establishment Clause decisions in the school prayer cases, that the issue was again pursued, culminating in the Supreme Court's 1968 decision in *Epperson v. Arkansas.*

The Scopes "Monkey Trial" Redux

Arkansas' anti-evolution statute, passed in 1928, was in practical effect identical to the Butler Act, making it a crime "to teach the theory or doctrine that mankind ascended or descended from a lower order of animals" or "to adopt or use in any such institution a textbook" that holds this view. No one had ever been prosecuted under the law, but the Arkansas Education Association sought to challenge it on Establishment Clause grounds and, ultimately, it convinced a high school teacher, Susan Epperson, to do so. The Arkansas Education Association brought a lawsuit in her name, seeking to have the law invalidated.

After a one-day trial, an Arkansas trial court judge ruled that the Arkansas law was unconstitutional, but the Arkansas attorney general appealed, and the Arkansas Supreme Court then reinstated the law as "a valid exercise of the state's power to specify the curriculum in its public schools." The Supreme Court accepted the appeal in order to finally settle the issue the Scopes "Monkey Trial" had raised but not resolved: whether states could ban the teaching of evolution in public schools, or whether such a ban was unconstitutional.

The result: a unanimous Supreme Court ruled that a ban on the teaching of evolution violates the Establishment Clause.

Justice Abraham Fortas, writing for the majority, explained that the Establishment Clause mandates that government maintain a position of neutrality in religious matters. "Government in our democracy, state and national, must be neutral in matters of religious theory, doctrine, and practice. It may not be hostile to any religion or to the advocacy of no-religion; and it may not aid, foster, or promote one religion or religious theory against another." Contrary to this tenet of law, the Court found that the sole reason for the Arkansas law was that a particular religious group considered the theory of evolution to be in conflict with the Bible's account of creation, a view that group favored. As a result, the Court ruled that "Arkansas' law cannot be defended as an act of religious neutrality."

The Evolution of the Creationists

Creationists responded with a switch in tactics. Rather than outlawing the teaching of evolution altogether, they successfully passed "equal time" or "balanced treatment" statutes that mandated that both evolution and "creation science" be taught. The rationale for these laws, went the argument, was that the teaching of various scientific theories would advance the cause of science instruction generally, which was a secular, nonreligious purpose beyond the reach of the Establishment Clause.

These efforts eventually found their way to the Supreme Court, in the 1987 decision in *Edwards v. Aguillard*, which directly confronted the issue of whether "creation science" was really science, or religion in scientific clothing. Seventy-two Nobel Prize–winning scientists, seventeen state academies of science, and seven other scientific organizations urged that "creation science" was, in fact, religion.

By a 7–2 majority, the Supreme Court agreed. The Court found that "the term 'creation science' . . . embodies the religious belief that a supernatural creator was responsible for the creation of humankind." This, said the Court, documented that "creation science" had as its primary purpose the advancement of a particular religious viewpoint— that is, the belief in a supreme being—and was therefore at odds with the Establishment Clause.

The Edwards decision, however, was equally unsuccessful in ending these confrontations. After Edwards, opponents of the teaching of evolution promoted the concept of "intelligent design" as a curriculum that could be taught in the public schools without offending the Establishment Clause. "Intelligent design" points to gaps in the theory of evolution, contends that nature exhibits a "purposeful arrangement of parts," and posits that an "intelligent designer" must therefore have been involved in creation generally and mankind in particular—but does not go so far as to state directly that the "intelligent designer" must be God.

The constitutionality of teaching "intelligent design" is being actively litigated in the lower courts. Almost inevitably, the proponents and opponents of "intelligent design" will eventually find their way to the Supreme Court, where yet another chapter of the book that began with the Scopes "Monkey Trial" will be written.

5. Van Orden v. Perry

6. McCreary County, Kentucky v. ACLU of Kentucky

The Ten Commandments Cases:
Religion in the Public Square 2005

The school prayer and creationism cases provided substantial clarity to the dispute over religion in the public schools. But what about religion in the public square?

In two Supreme Court cases decided in 2005, the Supreme Court determined whether state-sponsored displays of the Ten Commandments violate the Establishment Clause. In these cases, *Van Orden v. Perry* and *McCreary County, Kentucky v. ACLU of Kentucky*, the Supreme Court has revealed much about where, and how, it will draw the boundaries between church and state in the years to come.

Approximately forty years ago, a patriotic organization presented Texas with a six-foot monolith inscribed with the Ten Commandments. Texas chose to display the monument on state land at state expense, between the Texas State Capitol and the Texas Supreme Court, among approximately twenty other monuments of varying types and themes. More recently, two Kentucky counties posted large, highly visible copies of the Ten Commandments in their courthouses.

Both displays were challenged in court—the *Van Orden* case arose out of the Texas display, and the *McCreary* case arose out of the Kentucky display. The issue in both cases was whether displaying the Ten Commandments on public property brought church and state too close together, in violation of the Establishment Clause. The Supreme

Court, seeking an opportunity to clarify how separate church and state must be, agreed to hear the appeals of these cases.

By a 5–4 margin, the Court ruled that some intermixture between church and state is permissible, and that the Texas display did not violate the Establishment Clause. However, the Court also ruled that too much intermixture is impermissible, and that the Kentucky display did violate the Establishment Clause. Where is the line, and how does one find it?

To resolve these issues, the *McCreary* and *Van Orden* cases relied on a sometimes-discredited 1971 Supreme Court decision, *Lemon v. Kurtzman*, which gave birth to what is known in constitutional law circles as the "*Lemon* test." According to the *Lemon* test, in order to satisfy the Establishment Clause government conduct must have a secular purpose, it must have a primary effect that neither advances nor inhibits religion, and it must not foster excessive government entanglement with religion. In most contexts, the *Lemon* test asks judges to determine if the *real* purpose and effect of a government action trends more toward the religious or more toward the secular.

The Texas Ten Commandments monument was part of a larger display that highlighted the role of both religious and secular influences in law, government, and history. Admittedly, the Ten Commandments is a religious icon; but, to the majority of the justices, the purpose and effect of the Texas Ten Commandments display was not primarily religious, in the sense of extolling the Ten Commandments for its spiritual content, but rather it focused on the historical and cultural role of the Ten Commandments in a larger, nonreligious context. The 5–4 majority allowed the Texas monument to stand for these reasons.

But the same could not be said about the Kentucky display. The Ten Commandments display was put there by itself, within no larger historic or cultural context, and for no apparent purpose other than to endorse the Ten Commandments for its own sake. Because there was no independent, secular reason to justify the display of a religious symbol, the 5–4 majority required that the Kentucky display be removed.

How Much Religion Is Too Much Religion?

What do the *McCreary* and *Van Orden* decisions bode for the future of church–state relationships?

The fact that the Supreme Court will not mandate anything approaching a total "separation of church and state" was a foregone conclusion; after all, as has been the tradition for many years, every Supreme Court session begins with a Supreme Court official intoning "God save the United States and this Honorable Court," and it is not likely that the "In God We Trust" inscription will be removed from the money supply any time soon.

But, importantly, *McCreary* and *Van Orden* confirm the ground rules by which future church–state issues will be analyzed and decided. Judicial conservatives have for many years believed that the *Lemon* test unlawfully restricts the role of religion in American life, and they have argued, often passionately, for its elimination from our church–state jurisprudence. Justice Scalia has written (as only he can) that, implicitly if not explicitly, prior Supreme Court decisions had already overruled the *Lemon* test and, yet, it continues to live, like "some ghoul in a late-night horror movie that repeatedly sits up in its grave and shuffles abroad, after repeatedly being killed and buried." *McCreary* and *Van Orden* establish that, as the saying goes, the rumors of the *Lemon* test's demise have been greatly exaggerated.

This sets the stage for the Supreme Court's next, and very difficult, phase of church–state rulings. Are government grants that support "faith-based" organizations constitutional? What about challenges to the phrase "under God" in the Pledge of Allegiance that school children are often required to recite? What about the teaching of "intelligent design" as part of the science curriculum in public schools? *McCreary*'s and *Van Orden*'s reinvigoration of the *Lemon* test explains the theoretical line between constitutional and unconstitutional that will be used to decide these and similar issues: government support of religion primarily for the sake of religion itself will be prohibited, but many other forms of government involvement with religion will be permitted (though not to the extent Justice Scalia and many others would prefer).

The question, however, is where, exactly, this line will be placed, and which side of the church–state conundrum will be favored. More than anything else, the answer will be defined by who sits on the Court when these issues are confronted in the future. The *McCreary* and *Van Orden* decisions illuminate just how important one justice can be. Four justices (Rehnquist Scalia, Kennedy, and Thomas) voted to uphold both displays, and four justices (Stevens, O'Connor, Souter, and Ginsburg) voted to invalidate both displays. Justice Breyer was the swing vote: he believed that the Texas display was constitutional and that the Kentucky display was unconstitutional, accounting for the 5–4 vote in each case. As a practical matter, Justice Breyer, himself, defined the present boundary line between constitutional and unconstitutional.

As of this writing, three of the justices who sat on the *McCreary* and *Van Orden* cases (Rehnquist, O'Connor, and Souter) are no longer on the Court. If *McCreary* and *Van Orden* came before today's Court, would a five-vote coalition that disagreed with Justice Breyer's interpretation emerge? Where might future Courts, comprised of different justices, place the boundary line?

Each Supreme Court justice's experience and values influence how precedent is interpreted and applied, especially when it comes to incendiary issues like the relationship between church and state. There is a human element that cannot be removed from these equations. As the roster of justices change, so might the legal precepts that guide our way.

CHAPTER 3

INNOCENT UNTIL PROVEN GUILTY: THE RIGHTS OF THE ACCUSED

*"Better that ten guilty persons escape
than that one innocent suffer."*

—WILLIAM BLACKSTONE,
EIGHTEENTH-CENTURY ENGLISH JURIST

Our Founding Fathers were mindful of the penchant of monarchs to charge persons with false crimes as a means of political oppression and social control. Consequently, they built copious protections for those accused of criminal offenses into the foundations of the Constitution. It was acknowledged that giving all benefits of the doubt to the accused would result in some guilty persons being set free, and yet they freely accepted this necessary evil as a price of freedom.

The story is told of a Chinese law professor who was advised of our belief that it was better that a thousand guilty men go free than one innocent man be executed.

The Chinese professor thought for a bit and asked, "Better for whom?"

The Founding Fathers' answer to that question was this: better for all, because as history has proven, if anyone can be unlawfully jailed, everyone can be unlawfully jailed.

A witness stand in the Plymouth, Massachusetts County Court House, 1966.

7. Gideon v. Wainwright

The Right to Be Represented by Counsel
when Charged with a Crime 1963

The Sixth Amendment to the Constitution provides that in criminal prosecutions, the accused has the right "to have the Assistance of Counsel for his defence." Based on this constitutional mandate, federal courts have for many years appointed lawyers for criminal defendants who are without the means to hire a lawyer on their own. However, until the 1960s, the law was unclear as to whether the Sixth Amendment also applied to the states, where the vast majority of criminal prosecutions took place. As a result, the Supreme Court left it to each state to decide for itself whether indigent defendants charged in state courts would be provided with lawyers—and this resulted in innumerable unrepresented people being convicted of crimes they claimed they had not committed.

In 1961, Clarence Gideon was accused of robbing a pool hall in Florida, and was charged with various crimes in a Florida state court. Gideon could not afford a lawyer, and at his trial he asked the judge to appoint a lawyer for him so that, as promised by the Sixth Amendment, he could have the assistance of counsel. The judge refused, in compliance with Florida law at the time, and Gideon was left to defend himself. Gideon maintained that he was innocent but, unschooled in the law, he did not do a good job defending himself at his trial. He was convicted and sentenced to five years in jail.

Gideon's Trumpet

From his jail cell, Gideon wrote out a petition to the Supreme Court of the United States. Gideon's position was simply this: an individual's ability to exercise his constitutional rights, in this case his Sixth Amendment right to have the assistance of counsel, should not depend on his wealth, or anything else. All Americans should have the same constitutional rights, in theory and in practice.

The Supreme Court agreed to hear Gideon's appeal. At the root of the case was this issue: could a defendant in a criminal case conceivably get a fair trial without the assistance of a lawyer?

In its decision, the Supreme Court detailed the extent to which our courts are subject to specialized procedures and rules, and the fact that the knowledge and skill required to assemble and conduct a defense take years of training and experience to acquire. As a result, the Court reasoned, "The right to be heard would be, in many cases, of little avail if it did not comprehend the right to be heard by counsel." Without counsel, the Court concluded, an innocent defendant "faces the danger of conviction because he does not know how to establish his innocence."

On these bases, the Supreme Court invalidated Gideon's conviction, ordered a retrial, and required that a lawyer be appointed to defend him. At his new trial, with the help of a lawyer, Gideon was acquitted of the crime.

Fifty years ago, it was routine for indigent persons to be charged with crimes and forced to defend themselves in state courts without the assistance of a lawyer; that scenario is now constitutionally unimaginable. Clarence Gideon changed the law, inspiring the book and movie *Gideon's Trumpet* (with Henry Fonda playing Gideon). As Robert F. Kennedy put it, "If an obscure Florida convict named Clarence Earl Gideon had not sat down in his prison cell . . . to write a letter to the Supreme Court . . . the vast machinery of American law would have gone on functioning undisturbed. But Gideon did write that letter, the Court did look into his case . . . and the whole course of American legal history has been changed."

8. Miranda v. Arizona

"You Have the Right to Remain Silent . . .":
The Privilege Against Self-Incrimination 1966

Consider this situation. A kidnapping and sexual assault occurs. The police arrest a suspect and take him to the police station, where he is identified by the victim. In accordance with standard operating procedures, the suspect is then taken into a private interrogation room. The suspect is not advised that he has the right to be represented by a lawyer before he is questioned. Two hours later, the suspect signs a confession. There is no evidence that the suspect was physically or mentally abused in any way. The confession includes a statement that the suspect has "full knowledge of my legal rights, understanding any statement I make may be used against me," and that he had knowingly waived those rights. The suspect is put on trial, the confession is read to the jury, and the suspect is convicted.

Anything wrong with that?

These are the basic facts in the famous *Miranda* case, decided in 1966, in which the Supreme Court, in a 5–4 decision, ruled that once Ernesto Miranda was taken into police custody and before any interrogation could begin, the police had the constitutional duty under the Fifth Amendment to advise him that he had the right to refuse to answer any questions and to be represented by a lawyer, and if Miranda chose to take advantage of those rights, the police could not interrogate him in any way. Because the police failed to advise Miranda of these rights—now known as "Miranda rights"—before they questioned him and obtained his confession, Miranda's conviction was thrown out, just as innumerable convictions since the *Miranda* decision have been thrown out for similar reasons.

Taking the Fifth

The Fifth Amendment to the Constitution commands that no person "shall be compelled in any criminal case to be a witness against himself." As fundamental as this right is, however, it has an image problem. The Fifth Amendment is popularly viewed as a "legal technicality"—a loophole guilty people can use in their effort to beat the system. In television and movies, street-savvy punks and sophisticated white-collar criminals smugly refuse to answer questions in the police station, while they mock the detectives' impotence. The evening news televises congressional hearings in which reputed organized-crime figures and alleged corporate looters mechanically recite,"I assert my Fifth Amendment right against self-incrimination."

But the Fifth Amendment is anything but a legal technicality or a loophole.

It is easier and quicker for law-enforcement authorities to solve a crime by coercing a confession than it is to solve a crime through tedious investigation, particularly where the evidence may be hard to come by. In the seventeenth century, this fact of life led to horrific injustices in England (and elsewhere), in which innocent people were jailed on the basis of confessions made only after physical abuse or threats of harm. In reaction (some say revolution) against these wrongs, the right against self-incrimination—that is, the right to make law enforcement prove its case without the testimony of the suspect— became entrenched as a bedrock principle of English law. The Founding Fathers brought this precept with them to the colonies. They knew the horrors of the Old World too well and resolved to build the right against self-incrimination into the framework of the Constitution.

Still, the issue the Supreme Court faced in *Miranda* was different. By the time the *Miranda* case arose, it was a given that the police could not coerce a suspect to confess and then use that confession against him. And even Miranda's lawyers did not argue that anyone had coerced a confession out of Miranda: he was put into an interrogation room, confronted by the police, and after a couple of hours of questioning he signed a statement.

Ignorance of the Law Can Be an Excuse

The Supreme Court ruled that this was not enough to protect Miranda's Fifth Amendment rights. It reviewed the many studies showing how subtle, psychological techniques can be used to intimidate unsophisticated suspects into signing an untrue confession. The Fifth Amendment, said the Court, prohibits much more than beatings with rubber hoses and the "third degree."

More important, the Supreme Court ruled that the Fifth Amendment is so crucial that law-enforcement officials must make certain that a suspect is aware of the right to remain silent and the right to counsel, before any questioning can take place—and the rule applies not only when the police seek to directly question a suspect, but also when they try to elicit incriminating evidence through intimidation or manipulation techniques. If the suspect then intelligently and voluntarily waives his rights, so be it, but you cannot waive a right until you know that the right exists, and it is up to law enforcement to make certain that persons in their custody have this knowledge. Otherwise, said the Court, the potential for abuse is far greater than is tolerable in a civilized society.

After Miranda was decided, television viewers and moviegoers were routinely treated to chase scenes in which sprinting police officers tackle desperate criminals, at which time one of the officers triumphantly instructs an underling, "Read him his rights" ("You have the right to remain silent, anything you say can and will be used against you in a court of law . . .").

In this context, Miranda rights seem formulaic and silly, and it is easy to ignore their true significance. But the message of the case is of colossal importance: every individual accused of a crime has the right and the power to require that the government prove its accusations through real, substantive evidence, and every individual is provided with safeguards, like a lawyer and an unbiased court, to fend off the ability of those in power to get you if they want to.

As for Ernesto Miranda himself, his confession was thrown out. The police assembled the evidence, retried him, and Miranda was convicted.

CHAPTER 4

THE MELTING POT: RACE, DISCRIMINATION, AND DIVERSITY

"The one place where a man ought to get a square deal is in a courtroom, be he any color of the rainbow . . ."

—ATTICUS FINCH,
IN *To Kill a Mockingbird* BY HARPER LEE

It has often been observed that the history of America is in many ways the history of race relations. The Supreme Court has written much of that history, often with regrettable results. Ultimately, however, the Court turned prior law on its head, declared racial segregation unconstitutional, and literally changed America. The resulting anti-discrimination inertia not only led to expanded rights for minorities; it also launched anti-discrimination efforts in many other contexts, such as gender, age, religion, nationality, and sexual orientation, to name a few.

But here's the complication. Where is the line between prohibiting discrimination *against* individuals based on, for instance, their race or nationality, and *favoring* individuals based on their race or nationality? Isn't that discrimination in reverse? And what about the right of people to be left alone? If they want to associate only with people of their own race, or gender, or sexual orientation, should the law be able to stop them?

Vivian Malone, one of the first African Americans to attend the University of Alabama, walks through a crowd that includes photographers, National Guard members, and Deputy U.S. Attorney General Nicholas Katzenbach, June 11, 1963.

9. Brown v. Board
of Education

Separate Is Not Equal:
The End of Legalized Segregation 1954

The aftermath of slavery plagued the twentieth century, as segregation remained a practical reality throughout much of the North, and was mandated by state and local laws throughout the South. Blacks attempted to challenge segregation in the courts, but in 1896, in the case of *Plessy v. Ferguson*, the Supreme Court openly endorsed the concept of "separate but equal." On the basis of that precedent, local courts, as well as the Supreme Court itself, repeatedly refused to rule that segregation in education (or anything else) was unconstitutional.

In the 1930s, the NAACP developed a legal strategy to challenge the "separate but equal" concept: in one school after another, it successfully showed that the separate educational facilities being provided to blacks were not equal, and were in fact vastly inferior. By the 1950s, however, the NAACP's legal team—led by Thurgood Marshall, later to serve as the Supreme Court's first black justice—concluded that it would take decades to effect real change by challenging segregation on a case-by-case basis. Instead, the decision was made to challenge the "separate but equal" doctrine of *Plessy v. Ferguson* head-on. *Brown v. Board of Education* was the result.

The NAACP lawyers' argument was simply this: segregated schools were inherently unequal and could not be made equal, and forcing blacks to attend such schools violated the constitutional guaranty of equal protection under law. The NAACP contended, through the testimony of social scientists, that segregation itself was the problem: no matter how good the buildings, teachers, and curriculum might be, segregation, by its very nature, diminished the self-esteem and educational development of black children.

The Supreme Court Rules . . . and Society Changes

The case was argued in the Supreme Court for a remarkable six days (usually, each side is limited to about an hour), and in a unanimous opinion brokered through the arduous efforts of Chief Justice Warren, the Supreme Court adopted the NAACP's position. "Segregation of white and colored children in public schools has a detrimental effect upon the colored children," the chief justice wrote in the Court's opinion, and the detriment is even "greater when it has the sanction of law, for the policy of segregating the races is usually interpreted as denoting the inferiority of the Negro group." Overruling more than a half century of precedent, Warren plainly stated that the doctrine of "separate but equal" has no place in American education—and, by implication, anywhere else in America.

But, having so ruled, the Court was left to decide what to do about segregated schools. Chief Justice Warren felt that he could not set a timetable for desegregation, and instead ruled that children must be admitted to public schools without regard for their race "with all deliberate speed." That now-famous phrase led to hundreds of local court challenges to desegregation measures in both the North and South, and even the use of federal troops to enforce local court desegregation decisions. But after enduring one of the most explosively divisive episodes in American history, by the early 1970s almost half of all black children in the South attended predominantly white schools—a higher percentage of desegregation than existed in the North.

As significant as the desegregation of public schools has proven to be, the reach of *Brown v. Board of Education* extends much further. The case sparked a firestorm of protests while at the same time creating much of the impetus for the Civil Rights Act of 1964; it spurred a string of later decisions that eliminated the legal underpinnings for other aspects of segregation in American life; and it laid much of the groundwork for the civil rights movement that continues today. Many legal commentators consider *Brown v. Board of Education* to be the most significant Supreme Court decision of the twentieth century.

10. Gratz v. Bollinger

11. Grutter v. Bollinger

Can One Race Be Favored over Another Race in the Name of Diversity? 2003

Should Your Race *Ever* Matter?

In the 1990s, the University of Michigan utilized an admissions policy in its undergraduate school that assigned a predetermined number of points to various admissions criteria, such as grades, standardized test scores, quality of high school, residence, legacy status, and so on: the higher the point total, the greater the chance that an applicant would be admitted. The university wished to increase the diversity of its student population in order to serve its educational objectives and, therefore, it also added points to an applicant's admissions score if the applicant was a member of certain minority or racial groups that were underrepresented on campus. As the system existed in 1999, applicants who were members of these minority or racial groups would receive twenty extra points. This was significant—applicants with at least one hundred points were automatically admitted.

At about the same time, the University of Michigan Law School also sought to achieve diversity in its student body. However, in its admission process, the law school did not use a points system: rather, it considered the usual factors (grades, standardized tests, recommendations, and so on), and also a variety of subjective and nontraditional criteria, one of which being whether the applicant would increase diversity. The law school did not limit its diversity goals to race or ethnicity—it also sought, for instance, geographic and economic diversity—but it did admit that it actively sought a "critical mass" of minority students.

Two well-qualified white Michigan residents who were denied admission as undergraduates, and one well-qualified white Michigan resident who was denied admission to the law school, filed suit against the university's president, claiming that they had been discriminated against on the basis of their race in violation of the Constitution and the Civil Rights Act of 1964. Ultimately, in 2003, these "reverse discrimination" cases ended up in the Supreme Court: *Gratz v. Bollinger* (dealing with the university's undergraduate admission policy), and *Grutter v. Bollinger* (dealing with the university's law-school admission policy).

The Supreme Court's Balancing Act

The issue involved the collision of two worthy goals. One goal was the avoidance of racism in any form. As a fundamental, bedrock principle, discrimination on the basis of race is unlawful. In America, we are to be judged by our qualifications, not our color. The other goal was diversification in our educational institutions. For all sorts of reasons, going as far back as *Brown v. Board of Education*, the Supreme Court agreed with the educators, sociologists, and other experts who concluded that "separate but equal" does not work, and diverse student bodies foster excellence in education.

But how can you increase diversity in a student body without considering the race of those you are considering for admission into that student body?

The Supreme Court justices were bitterly divided over how best to balance these competing goals. Rather than speaking in one voice, the vote was split, and even those justices who agreed on the result wrote separate opinions expressing different rationales. But out of this confusion, a portentous message emerged.

In the *Gratz* case, involving the University of Michigan undergraduate school, the Court found the admissions procedure to be unconstitutional, by a 6–3 margin. Any consideration of race must be very narrowly tailored, the Court ruled, and automatically awarding points for minority status was analogous to a quota system, and was over the line.

But in the *Grutter* case, involving the University of Michigan Law School, the Court ruled otherwise, although by only a 5–4 margin. It found that by reviewing each student individually (and less mechanically), and by crediting diversity factors aside from just race, the racial aspects of the admissions criteria had been sufficiently narrowed to satisfy constitutional requirements.

Color Blind No More?

This conclusion is of monumental significance. In the *Grutter* case, a majority of the Court crossed what had been a virtually impenetrable racial divide: the Supreme Court ruled that color blindness is no longer legally mandated in America, and that racial favoritism (the other side of which is racial discrimination) can be legal, in narrowly defined circumstances: as part of an overall assessment of an applicant's qualifications, an applicant's race can be considered as one of many factors in pursuit of a compelling social interest—in this case, diversity in an educational institution.

The remaining issue is how far the *Grutter* rationale will be taken in the future. Could it be used to justify more than just diversity—for instance, what about school districts that seek to achieve goals they believe to be equally worthy, such as racial balance?

Outside of the educational arena, could it be used to legalize other kinds of racial favoritism? For instance, if studies show that, for instance, police departments and high school faculties are more effective if they mimic the racial makeup of the communities they serve, can race be considered in police and faculty hiring decisions?

What about the business world generally? Justice Sandra Day O'Connor, who wrote the majority opinion in *Grutter*, justified her conclusion, at least in part, on the basis of practical considerations. Justice O'Connor observed that "American businesses have made clear that the skills needed in today's increasingly global marketplace can only be developed through exposure to widely diverse people, cultures, ideas, and viewpoints." It is not difficult to imagine the arguments this logic will lead to in the future. If race can be used as a law school admissions criterion in order to serve the practical purpose of helping the university achieve its diversity goals, why can't it be used as a business hiring criterion for the practical purpose of helping a business achieve its financial goals? For instance, if a company does business in Asia and will be more successful with its Asian customers and suppliers if it employs more Asian executives and salespeople, can it favor Asians over whites in the hiring process? And, ultimately, if an American company does business mainly with foreign companies who favor whites, could that be used by the American company as a justification to favor whites over minorities in its hiring process?

Lower courts have only recently begun the process of analyzing these kinds of issues, but in the interim, the Supreme Court (having undergone some key departures and replacements since *Grutter* was decided) has sent out some signals that will strongly influence the direction in which future decisions will likely trend. In particular, in 2007, the Supreme Court invalidated two school district programs that considered race when assigning students to schools. One of the programs was designed to maintain racial mixtures that roughly paralleled the larger community; the other was intended to maintain prior desegregation efforts; both programs were found to be constitutionally infirm. The message seems to be that, barring significant changes in the Court's makeup, future decisions will most likely narrow, not broaden, the circumstances in which race can be considered, and the methods by which racial data may be utilized.

What all of this portends for the future of public policies that include a racial component (educational diversity, workplace hiring procedures, affirmative action, and so on) is a hugely important issue that is analyzed in the last chapter of this book. Having started down the road of addressing these issues, the Supreme Court will be asked to resolve the many uncertainties that remain, as more litigants test the boundaries of the *Gratz* and *Grutter* decisions. Whether this opens a floodgate, or merely a faucet, remains to be seen.

12. Boy Scouts of America v. Dale

The Right of "Expressive Association"—Free Speech or Legalized Discrimination? 2000

James Dale, a college student in New Jersey, had been a Boy Scout since he was twelve. He applied for a scoutmaster position and was accepted. Shortly thereafter, Dale openly acknowledged that he was gay; and after a newspaper wrote an article featuring Dale's involvement in a gay-rights group, the Boy Scouts of America revoked his membership, based on his sexual orientation.

Truly private clubs can usually admit, or not admit, whoever they want. But in many cases, organizations that are generally open to the public are treated differently. In the case of New Jersey, like many states it had enacted a statute prohibiting discrimination on the basis of sexual orientation (among other characteristics, such as race and religion) by establishments (like restaurants and office buildings) and organizations (like the Boy Scouts) that usually admit just about anyone who walks through the door.

Dale sued the Boy Scouts, claiming that his rights under the New Jersey law had been violated. The Boy Scouts, on the other hand, argued that the New Jersey law violated its constitutional rights. We are entitled to our own standards and preferences, the Boy Scouts argued, and no state should have the right to tell us what to do about our own membership.

The Boy Scouts won in the trial court, but Dale won an appeal to the New Jersey Supreme Court. The Boy Scouts then appealed to the U.S. Supreme Court, resulting in the case of *Boy Scouts of America v. Dale.*

The Freedom Not to Associate

In prior cases, the Supreme Court had ruled that even in the face of anti-discrimination statutes like New Jersey's, certain types of otherwise open-door associations do have a right to restrict their membership in certain circumstances. The First Amendment guarantees the people the freedom to associate with whomever they please. But, said the Court, there is also a freedom not to associate, even in the face of a contrary law, among certain kinds of groups. The Supreme Court calls these groups "expressive associations," meaning associations that promote certain values or points of view, like an association that promotes good citizenship or the importance of buying American-made goods. In that kind of a group, said the Court, the members' First Amendment rights of free speech could be compromised if the government were permitted to force them to accept people who opposed what the group stood for: picture an association whose mission is to promote unionization being forced to admit members who are anti-union.

But there are limits to how exclusive such expressive associations may be. In 1984, the Supreme Court decided a case, *Roberts v. United States Jaycees*, which explained how these conflicts are to be analyzed and resolved.

The *Roberts* case involved the Jaycees, or Junior Chamber of Commerce, a national civic organization that, at the time, restricted full voting membership to males between the ages of eighteen and thirty-five. Minnesota had an anti-discrimination law similar to New Jersey's, and a lawsuit was brought against the Jaycees seeking to invalidate their male-only policy.

The majority of the Supreme Court justices felt that the Jaycees were an expressive association, but the Jaycees lost anyway and were required to admit women. The rationale for the Supreme Court's decision was simple: admitting women into the Jaycees would not compromise the free speech rights of the Jaycees' membership, because the admission of women had nothing to do with the Jaycees' mission or message. The Jaycees promoted, for instance, community service and the development of business skills, and they could do just as good a job discussing and promoting those messages if women were members. Because the Jaycees' free speech rights would not be affected by enforcing the Minnesota law against it, the Supreme Court ruled that the Jaycees were required to abide by the law.

Dale argued that the same logic should apply to the Boy Scouts. Dale was more than qualified to be a scoutmaster, and he firmly believed in everything the Boy Scouts stood for. The fact that he happened to be gay, he argued, should have no more relevance than if he were black.

Unlike the Jaycees, however, the Boy Scouts won its case, although by only a 5–4 vote, and were permitted to exclude Dale solely because of his sexual orientation. Chief Justice Rehnquist wrote the opinion for the majority.

Rehnquist found that, like the Jaycees, the Boy Scouts was an expressive association entitled to First Amendment protection because it sought to transfer faith-based values, such as those in the Scout Oath and Scout Law, from adult members to youth members. Those values stressed the importance of being "morally straight" and "clean," and the Boy Scouts argued, without proof and based solely on the views of the organization's leadership, that homosexuals were not role models consistent with those precepts. If forced to allow homosexuals to serve as scoutmasters, the Boy Scouts contended, it would be forced to implicitly endorse a point of view with which it did not agree.

At the same time, however, the Boy Scouts admitted that none of the values it promoted mentioned anything about sexual orientation, and it had no evidence that gays in general, or Dale in particular, would do anything to interfere with the teaching of the Scout Oath or Scout Law. The Boy Scouts' case depended solely on its opinion about homosexuality in general: in the view of the Boy Scouts, merely being a homosexual was inconsistent with morality.

Rehnquist ruled that the Boy Scouts was entitled to its opinion. While stressing that the Supreme Court was not endorsing or agreeing with the Boy Scouts' view, Rehnquist concluded that it was not up to the Court to dictate what positions the Boy Scouts should espouse. Under the First Amendment, he ruled, the Boy Scouts could not be compelled to accept a scoutmaster if, in the Boy Scouts' view, the message the organization wanted to send to its members would be compromised.

Expressive Association versus Unlawful Discrimination: Now What?

The *Boy Scouts* decision is about much more than whether the Boy Scouts could be compelled to accept a gay scoutmaster.

As a society, we stand for the proposition that all men are created equal. This bedrock precept finds its roots in the Equal Protection Clause of the Constitution; its implementation was jumpstarted by one of the most acclaimed Supreme Court decisions, *Brown v. Board of Education*; and it has since been codified in extensive federal, state, and local anti-discrimination laws. As a preeminent social prerogative, we seek a society where certain characteristics—for example, race, religion, nationality, gender, disability, and in some states, sexual orientation— will not compromise the rights and privileges of the people who live here. Toward that end, we have established laws forbidding discrimination on the basis of these characteristics.

How, then, could the Boy Scouts escape their obligation to obey a state law that prohibits discrimination against gays? The right of expressive association on which the case was pinioned was crystallized by the Supreme Court in the 1950s and 1960s, when civil rights organizations sought to protect themselves from being overrun and dominated by an influx of those who unashamedly sought to promote a racist agenda. The Boy Scouts, however, faced no such threat. They were allowed to exclude gays and in the process violate an anti-discrimination law based solely on the opinion of the Boy Scouts' leadership that homosexuality was inherently immoral and, therefore, counter to the organizational mission. When you are talking about allowing an organization to violate an otherwise valid law, shouldn't it take more than an opinion?

Suppose the Jaycees had taken the position that, in its opinion, women are not civic-minded and, therefore, their mere presence would negate the message the Jaycees tried to promote to its membership? Would the Jaycees have been permitted to exclude women on that rationale, without any evidence? What if an expressive organization that promotes business ethics refused to accept foreigners or minorities because, in the bigoted opinion of the organization's leaders, all foreigners and minorities are unethical?

The *Boy Scouts* decision arguably elevates the right of expressive association to the status of a full-fledged First Amendment right, the kind of right that generally takes priority over other, conflicting rights, and this raises implications that are potentially monumental. In his dissent to Chief Justice Rehnquist's opinion, for instance, Justice Souter wrote that the decision made the right of expressive association "an easy trump of any anti-discrimination law."

For example, in the *Gratz* and *Grutter* cases explained earlier in this chapter, the University of Michigan sought to justify favoring racial minorities as part of a plan to increase diversity. The Supreme Court was, to say the least, skeptical. But suppose the University had taken a different tack—suppose it argued that the University was an expressive association that stood for pluralism and the creation of an environment inclusive of racially diverse points of view? If the Boy Scouts' rights as an expressive association trumped its obligations to comply with anti-discrimination laws, why wouldn't a University's?

Housing discrimination is categorically unlawful. But after the *Boy Scouts* decision, could a developer market a "whites only" condominium development or apartment building for persons who believe in white supremacy? If the Boy Scouts have the constitutional right to exclude protected groups from their organization, why wouldn't the occupants of a building be entitled to form their own race-based association for the purpose of excluding minorities? Could unions, or charter schools, or country clubs exclude certain nationalities in the face of federal or state laws to the contrary based on the opinions of their leadership?

The *Boy Scouts* case stands for the proposition that organizations whose members focus on and promote a certain set of beliefs have the sacred First Amendment right to define their own membership rules, even if those rules violate anti-discrimination laws. The case defines and endorses the constitutional right of such associations to engage in otherwise-unlawful discrimination, whether based on race, religion, nationality or any other protected characteristic. On the one hand, the *Boy Scouts* decision manifests a respect for personal freedom, unencumbered by governmental dictates. But on the other hand, it creates a substantial loophole in the legal framework through which the law has, for decades, attempted to implement its nondiscriminatory ideals.

It will remain for future Supreme Courts to determine if they wish to walk through the door the *Boy Scouts* decision has opened and, if so, where they will take the future of our anti-discrimination precepts and principles thereafter.

CHAPTER 5

PLAYING POLITICS

"Politics is too serious a matter to be left to the politicians."

—CHARLES DE GAULLE,
FORMER PRESIDENT OF FRANCE

Democracies gather legitimacy from the free and fair elections through which they choose their leaders. History documents that if the electoral process loses credibility, the fabric of a democracy quickly unravels. It follows that a responsible government must focus, almost above all else, on preserving the public's confidence in the bona fides of its elections.

Increasingly, however, Americans have come to believe that elections can be bought, not by (as in prior eras) paying voters to stuff the ballot box, but through the purchase of media time and campaign machinery in such quantities as will steamroller an opponent of lesser means. The Supreme Court has recognized the dangers in a money-based electoral process, and the task of finding solutions that are both workable and constitutional has just begun.

There are other powers, as well, that the Supreme Court can use to assure the sanctity of our elections—as it attempted to do, with horrifically mixed reviews, in the 2000 presidential election.

Voters line up on Election Day in Clarendon, Virginia, 1924, to vote for president. Calvin Coolidge won the election.

13. Buckley v. Valeo

Money Talks: Campaign Finance Reform and the First Amendment 1976

From 1989 to 2002, Enron and its employees gave almost $6 million in contributions to federal candidates and parties. Did it get anything for its money? That depends on who you ask, but there is no denying that Enron officials had remarkable access to a sizable array of elected and appointed officials; a great deal of the energy policies and legislation it sought were enacted; and persons who Enron touted to the government as good candidates to populate the agencies that regulated Enron often ended up in office.

Maybe the contributions had nothing to do with Enron's political success. But there is at least a rational reason to wonder whether they did—that is, whether government is for sale to big-money interests— and many feel that such doubts and suspicions can be cancerous to the credibility a democratic government requires. And the cancer may be spreading, as the news media unravel story after story of campaign contributions that, it is charged, bought special-interest legislation for those who could afford to pay the price.

Scandals like Enron have fueled the fight for campaign finance reform. It is up to Congress to determine what type of federal campaign finance reform, if any, is best for the country, but there is a catch. Before Congress may rationally approach that issue, it has to confront a monumental impediment—the Constitution.

All agree that political candidates have a First Amendment right of free speech to get their message out to as wide an audience as they can. In today's world, that means using the mass media, and that takes money. The constitutional issue that has plagued campaign finance reform is whether the government can lawfully stop people who support the message a candidate is trying to publicize from providing the candidate with the money needed to do the job. Isn't the First Amendment all about the right of the people to join together and speak out on issues of public importance?

The *Buckley* Decision: Hush, Money

In the case of *Buckley v. Valeo*, the Supreme Court tried to answer that question. The case was brought by a senatorial odd couple—conservative Senator James Buckley and liberal Senator Eugene McCarthy—to challenge a federal campaign law that regulated campaign contributions.

The Court ruled that the First Amendment does invalidate laws that restrict a candidate from spending however much of his own money he wants to spend on his own election campaign. In that context, said the Court, the money is closely tied to free speech because only by spending money can the candidate effectively communicate with the voters. If Ross Perot wants to spend $50 million of his own money on a presidential run, said the Court, more power to him.

But, said the majority in the *Buckley* Court, the same is not true in respect to political contributions, and the government can limit the amount of those contributions without offending the Constitution. Drawing a distinction many analysts believe to be logically nonexistent, the majority of the Court reasoned that contributions are not speech, even though most candidates cannot effectively speak without them and, therefore, contributions are not entitled to First Amendment protection.

There was, and still is, substantial disagreement among the justices regarding that proposition. For instance, Justice Clarence Thomas, writing in another case, put it succinctly: "A contribution, by amplifying the voice of the candidate, helps to ensure the dissemination of the messages that the contributor wishes to convey. . . . By depriving donors of their right to speak through the candidate, contribution limits relegate donors' points of view to less effective modes of communication."

Buckley's Offspring: McCain–Feingold

Buckley broke the First Amendment ice for campaign finance reform, but it included a major loophole: in dealing only with the issue of contributions made directly to a candidate, it implicitly permitted the type of contribution which came to be known as "soft money." Instead of contributing directly to a candidate, a contributor would make the check payable to a political party or an organization which, for instance, would fund television ads that would run incessantly during a hotly contested political campaign. Not coincidentally, the ads would focus on an issue that distinguished one candidate from the other in the campaign and, without mentioning names, one candidate would be boosted over the other through the expenditure of millions of dollars which, if given directly to the favored candidate, would have been starkly illegal.

To attack that loophole, senators John McCain, R-Ariz. and Russ Feingold, D-Wisc., sponsored and successfully passed massive legislation, colloquially known as McCain–Feingold but formally titled the "Bipartisan Campaign Reform Act" or "BCRA." BCRA seriously restricted "soft money" contributions, and fomented a well-funded, well-lawyered court challenge sponsored by a massive coalition of plaintiffs and pursued in the name of Senator Mitch McConnell.

In the 2003 case of *McConnell v. FEC* (Federal Election Commission), in a nearly 300-page opinion supported by a bare 5–4 majority, the Supreme Court upheld (with minor exceptions) the constitutionality of BCRA. Buckley had opened a First Amendment door through which Senators McCain and Feingold escaped.

In the *McConnell* decision, the justices acknowledged that the country's method of electing candidates through massive infusions of interest group money created the appearance, and often the reality, of corruption. A substantial number of commentators who make their living parsing Supreme Court decisions explain the *McConnell* decision this way: the majority of the justices felt that they had to find a way, any way, around the First Amendment in order to allow campaign finance reform to move forward.

The *McConnell* dissenters were unrelenting and defiant. Justice Scalia wrote that the ruling was "a sad day for freedom of speech." "Who could have imagined," he said, "the Court would smile with favor upon a law that cuts to the heart of what the First Amendment is meant to protect: the right to criticize the government." Justice Thomas was even more condemnatory: "The Court today upholds what can only be described as the most significant abridgments of the freedom of speech and association since the Civil War."

Buckley, followed by *McConnell*, might change the way Americans choose their elected officials. But it might not. The issue is far from dead, and those on both sides continue to fight the fight with remarkable zeal. While *Buckley* established the general proposition that campaign contributions can be limited, cases now pending raise the issue of how far those limitations can be taken, and whom those limitations may affect. And many believe that as the roster of Supreme Court justices changes, a new majority may quickly jettison the *Buckley* framework altogether.

The Supreme Court itself acknowledged in *McConnell* that those persons and organizations with the money and will to support political positions will continue to fund the fight to make their money talk. As the majority in the *McConnell* decision wrote, "We are under no illusion that BCRA—the Bipartisan Campaign Reform Act—will be the last congressional statement on the matter. Money, like water, will always find an outlet."

14. Davis v. FEC

Can an Election Be Bought? 2008

Riding *Buckley v. Valeo's* coattails, *McConnell v. FEC* validated the key provisions of BCRA and allowed Congress to regulate "soft money" campaign expenditures. The Supreme Court seemingly recognized that if a substantial slice of the electorate reasonably believes that moneyed special interests can buy an election, the shared beliefs ("of the people, by the people, for the people") that make our democracy possible will dissipate into shared suspicions.

But there is another way an election can be bought: a candidate can buy it himself, with his own money. Should we care about that? BCRA was focused on reducing the outside influences that can corrupt elected officials, but that sort of corruption is not an issue when an ultra-wealthy candidate foots the bill himself. So what's the problem?

Many believe the problem is this: we're supposed to elect those who are the best, not necessarily those who are the richest. There's no question about the fact that money influences elections—a massive, slickly produced media campaign coupled with a deeply funded grassroots organization can mask and overwhelm the true merits of a candidate. Do we really want government to become a millionaires' club? What happened to the concept of electing the most-qualified candidate, as opposed to the candidate who can buy the most media time?

Still, there's another side to that (literal and figurative) coin: in a country that, thankfully, holds its constitutionally guaranteed freedoms sacrosanct, should we allow the government to step in and tell someone how he's permitted to spend his own money—especially if he wants to spend it to promote his own free speech on important political issues, with the ultimate goal of serving the public in an elected office?

Buckley v. Valeo recognized that a cap on personal spending could open a very dangerous door, and declared such restrictions unconstitutional. Sure, money can influence elections, but maybe that's a risk worth taking when the overriding goal is the preservation of our most central and deep-seated liberties.

The Millionaire's Amendment

Congress confronted this issue head-on when it drafted BCRA, and it handled the conundrum in a very crafty way, through a provision that has come to be known as the "Millionaire's Amendment." A candidate will be permitted to spend as much of his own money as he wants, Congress said. As decided in *Buckley*, the Constitution demands no less. But there was a catch. Once that candidate's spending level reaches a certain threshold, Congress went on, donors to that candidate's opponent, and the opponent's political party, will be permitted to contribute more money than BCRA would otherwise allow. The more of his own money the candidate spends, the more BCRA's restrictions will be relaxed in order to allow his opponent, as the cliché goes, to level the playing field.

The Constitutional Challenge

The constitutionality of the Millionaire's Amendment was challenged in court by Jack Davis, a New York Democrat who unsuccessfully sought a seat in the House of Representatives. Davis spent several million dollars of his own money in the process, and was more than a little angered by the fact that, thanks to the Millionaire's Amendment, his opponent was permitted to raise substantially more money from outside contributors than the law usually allows. Davis contended that the law violated his free speech rights under the First Amendment and his right to equal protection under the Fifth Amendment. Why should my opponents be allowed to exceed the fundraising limits that apply to the rest of us, and use that money to blunt the effects of my free speech, simply because I wrote my own checks?

The Solicitor General of the United States, whose job it is to defend the constitutionality of challenged federal laws, argued against Davis's position. The government, he contended, has a compelling interest in minimizing the perception that congressional seats are for sale. Besides, he continued, the Millionaire's Amendment did nothing to restrict Davis's free speech rights—he could spend as much of his own money as he wanted in the effort to communicate his message to voters. Whether or not Davis likes or agrees with the Millionaire's Amendment, went the argument, he has no constitutional right to compel his opponent to operate at a monetary disadvantage.

The trial court that first heard the case ruled against Davis, and did so emphatically, seeing no merit in his contentions. Davis appealed, and the Supreme Court agreed to hear the case.

The Supreme Court Then
versus the Supreme Court Now

Between the time *McConnell v. FEC* was decided in 2003 and the time *Davis v. FEC* hit the Supreme Court docket in 2008, the judicial arithmetic had shifted. *McConnell*, which upheld the constitutionality of campaign finance reform, was decided by a 5–4 margin. Justice O'Connor co-wrote the majority opinion. By 2008, however, Justice O'Connor, along with Chief Justice Rehnquist (a campaign finance reform skeptic), had left the Court. They had been replaced by Chief

Justice John Roberts and Justice Samuel Alito: each was somewhat of an unknown quantity, but both seem disposed against the constitutionality of campaign finance reform. In effect, the Supreme Court campaign finance reform head count went from a probable 5–4 in favor to a probable 5–4 against.

Those probabilities turned into a reality for Davis: by a 5–4 vote, with Roberts and Alito joining the majority, the Supreme Court declared the Millionaire's Amendment unconstitutional.

Justice Alito wrote the majority opinion. He conceded that the prevention of corruption may well be a sound reason for Congress to stick its legislative nose into the country's political debate, but beyond that, he said, Congress had no business increasing some electoral advantages and decreasing others. Some candidates have money, some have wealthy supporters, some are celebrities, some have a well-known family name. "Leveling electoral opportunities," he wrote, "means making and implementing judgments about which strengths should be permitted to contribute to the outcome of an election." "It is a dangerous business," he warned, "for Congress to use the election laws to influence the voters' choices."

Justice Alito then confronted the argument that BCRA does not limit an individual's right to spend as much as he wants but, rather, merely allows his opponent to raise more money to preserve the fairness of the process. That does not carry the day, he ruled. The Millionaire's Amendment "imposes an unprecedented penalty" on a candidate who chooses to "robustly" (i.e., by spending tons of money) exercise his First Amendment rights, said Justice Alito, and that's unconstitutional. Crucially, he concluded that "an interest in leveling electoral opportunities for candidates of different personal wealth" is not sufficient to override these First Amendment issues—"doing so would have ominous implications for the voters' authority to evaluate the strengths of candidates competing for office."

So What?

There's a case to be made, either way, when Congress imposes one fundraising standard on "millionaires" and another on those who cannot afford to fund their campaigns out of their own pockets. But Justice Alito's opinion seems to question the constitutionality of virtually *any* effort, including an even-handed one, that tries to address the danger that personal wealth, and the media it can buy, can skew an election.

Consider the 2004 campaign of then-senatorial candidate Obama. His Illinois primary opponent, Blair Hull, spent over $20 million of his own money in the campaign, and built a substantial lead in the polls. Obama was supported by a number of wealthy donors, and the Millionaire's Amendment allowed him to raise more than $2 million more than BCRA otherwise permitted. Some scandals in the personal life of Obama's opponent emerged, and the extra money doubtlessly helped Obama take full advantage through additional media ads. As Obama's then finance director Claire Serdiuk later stated, the Millionaire's Amendment "really did a great job in what it set out to do: leveling the playing field."

According to Justice Alito (and the four justices who joined in his opinion), what the Millionaire's Amendment did for now-President Obama is unconstitutional.

Does Campaign Finance Reform Have a Future?

The *Davis v. FEC* decision seems to say that in a political campaign where one side has a natural advantage, such as having more money, it violates the First Amendment for Congress to try to even out the contest, unless the congressional action is targeted toward the prevention of corruption. Having more money, according to Justice Alito, merely allows a candidate to "robustly" exercise First Amendment rights, and it is not the business of government to restrict those rights. Justice Alito plainly telegraphed a mistrust of government, and perceived an inherent danger in allowing it to enter the realm of determining which electoral advantages will be allowed to stand, and which must be subject to a government-supervised leveling process.

As usually occurs in judicial opinions, Justice Alito stuck to the narrow issues before him and did not make generalized pronouncements. But legal precedents evolve, one flowing from another, based on analogy: if the facts and circumstances of a prior case are analogous to the facts and circumstances in a later case, the decision in the prior case will strongly influence, if not determine, the decision in the later case.

And that raises a key issue for the future: will the decision in *Davis v. FEC* inexorably lead to the reversal of *Buckley* and *McConnell*, and the judicial elimination of campaign finance reform itself? The significance of the *Davis* decision lies in the monumentally important seeds it planted. Whether those seeds will be allowed to flourish is a topic dealt with in more detail in the final chapter.

15. Bush v. Gore

Did the Supreme Court Play Politics in the 2000 Election? 2000

In the view of many, the Supreme Court elected George W. Bush the president of the United States.

After the ballots were counted in the November 7, 2000, presidential election, Al Gore led Bush in the popular vote, and Gore led the electoral-college vote by a 267–246 margin. Whoever reached 270 electoral votes would win the presidency. The only state still in play was Florida, whose 25 electoral votes would go to the candidate who won the Florida popular vote. The initial Florida vote count had Bush leading Gore, 2,909,135 votes to 2,907,351, but because the margin was less than 0.5 percent, Florida law required a machine recount. The machine recount reduced Bush's margin to a scant 327 votes.

Gore, as was his right according to Florida law, then requested a manual recount in four Florida counties. The law, however, mandated that the recount be completed in seven days. This led three of the counties to request more time to complete the manual recount, but Florida's secretary of state, Katherine Harris, believing that an extension would be unlawful, refused the request. Gore disagreed with Harris's position, filed a lawsuit, and the legal dispute that eventually became *Bush v. Gore* was born.

In short order, Gore's case was argued before the Florida Supreme Court, which issued an order requiring Harris to allow the requested extension, through November 26. Bush appealed that ruling to the U.S. Supreme Court, which requested certain clarifications before it would rule. In the interim, one of the counties, Miami-Dade, canceled its manual recount, stating that it could not complete the recount by the November 26 deadline.

On November 26, despite the incomplete recount, Harris certified Bush as the winner by only 537 votes—thereby awarding Bush Florida's 25 electoral votes, and the presidency.

On November 27, Gore filed another suit to contest the certified results of the election. He lost, and again appealed to the Florida Supreme Court which, on December 8, ordered a state-wide, manual recount. Bush again appealed to the U.S. Supreme Court, which issued an injunction stopping the statewide recount, pending its final decision.

On December 11, the Supreme Court heard oral arguments. Just sixteen hours later, with the presidency in the balance and the nation on the edge of its seat, the Court rendered its opinion.

Hanging Chads, Dimpled Chads, and Equal Protection

The Supreme Court tied most of its analysis to the Equal Protection Clause of the Fourteenth Amendment to the Constitution, which provides that "No State shall . . . deny to any person . . . the equal protection of the laws." In the wake of televised accounts of election commissioners squinting through magnifying glasses, some finding significance in "hanging chads," others being influenced by "dimpled chads," Bush argued that there was no uniform vote-counting standard among the various Florida counties and, therefore, two voters in different counties could mark their ballots in an identical manner, and one would be counted while the other would be disregarded. This, said Bush, was a denial of equal protection, and the recount should be halted on that basis.

Gore argued that equal protection does not require absolute uniformity, and because all of the Florida counties subscribed to one standard—trying to derive the intent of the voters who marked the ballots—the Equal Protection Clause was satisfied. Gore pointed out that every state uses a variety of different methods to record votes in different counties, ranging from optical scanners to punch cards. Therefore, said Gore, if Bush prevailed, from that day forward every state would have to implement a uniform system of voting in order to satisfy constitutional standards, which was neither required under the law, nor possible as a matter of stark reality.

The Supreme Court's decision was a hodgepodge of arcane legal reasoning and varying alliances among varying justices on varying points, but the upshot was that Bush won. Essentially, the majority of justices ruled that the different vote-counting techniques undertaken in the recount were constitutionally problematic. This meant that the manual recount had to cease, and the election results had to be certified as they existed prior to the recount. Bush assumed the presidency on the strength of that opinion.

The Criticism from Without, and from Within

Bush v. Gore touched off an immediate explosion of political commentary, although, not surprisingly, in most instances those politicians who favored the Court's reasoning were prior adherents of Bush or his philosophies, and vice versa.

In addition, constitutional law scholars quickly emerged from their ivory towers. While some supported the decision, those who garnered the most media attention vituperatively denounced the legal underpinnings of the *Bush v. Gore* decision, often charging that the justices voted their politics, not the law. American University law professor Jamin Raskin wrote in the *Washington Monthly* that *Bush v. Gore* was "quite demonstrably the worst Supreme Court decision in history," even worse than the infamous Dred Scott decision. Harvard law professor Laurence Tribe, one of the country's most respected constitutional scholars (and one of the attorneys who represented Gore), wrote that the Court's opinion "cannot be grounded in any previously recognizable form of equal protection doctrine." Another Harvard law professor, Randall Kennedy, labeled the decision a "hypocritical mishmash of ideas." Mincing no words on his view of why the majority ruled as it did, Sanford Levinson, a University of Texas law professor, wrote in *The Nation* that the decision was "easily explainable" as the decision of Republican justices intended "to assure the triumph of a fellow Republican who might not become president if Florida were left to its own legal process."

Perhaps most disturbing, however, was the fact that allegations of this type, charging nothing short of judicial corruption, were not limited to pundits and professors. In divisive matters of national importance that consume the nation's attention, the Supreme Court strives for a unanimous opinion in the effort to speak with one voice and promote national unity. When, as in *Bush v. Gore*, that cannot be achieved, Supreme Court justices will normally characterize their disagreements as good faith disputes over legal precedents or philosophy. Very rarely will they question each other's motives or integrity. In *Bush v. Gore*, however, Justice Stevens, one of the dissenters, used startling language to characterize his view of what the Court's majority had done. He wrote that the majority's position "can only lend credence to the most cynical appraisal of the work of judges throughout the land. It is confidence in the men and women who administer the judicial system that is the true backbone of the rule of law. Time will one day heal the wound to that confidence that will be inflicted by today's decision. One thing, however, is certain. Although we may never know with complete certainty the identity of the winner of this year's Presidential election, the identity of the loser is perfectly clear. It is the Nation's confidence in the judge as an impartial guardian of the rule of law."

In advance of the 2004 presidential election, many had predicted that whoever lost would challenge the results based on the *Bush v. Gore* ruling that disparate vote-counting procedures could violate the Equal Protection Clause, and that the nation would then be thrown into tumult. Obviously, that did not happen. Still, voter confidence in the electoral system—a linchpin of any democracy—has shown problematic and continuing weaknesses. According to a 2008 study by the Pew Research Center, only 57 percent of Americans were "very confident" that their votes will be counted accurately—down from 62 percent in 2004. About 10 percent of the voters expressed little confidence in our voting system.

The 2008 presidential election was not close enough to cause doubts about the outcome based on voting inaccuracies, but it is certainly foreseeable that another too-close-to-call vote could emerge in a future election, resulting in a *Bush v. Gore*–like lawsuit. In 2006, for example, a Court of Appeals declared unconstitutional the use of different voting technologies in different Ohio counties because under one system voters were given the opportunity to find and correct mistakes they made on their ballot before casting their vote, and in another system they were not given that opportunity. Until the Supreme Court says otherwise, the analytical framework endorsed by the majority in *Bush v. Gore* continues to bind lower courts, creating the potential for similar election challenges in the future.

Especially in view of the changing makeup of the Court since 2000, it is impossible to predict whether the Supreme Court itself will again delve into the electoral process, or instead leave it to the states to untangle their own messes (as the dissenting justices argued the Court should have done in 2000). Justice Scalia has since expressed the view that *Bush v. Gore* is old news. When asked about the continuing penchant of many to decry the decision, his response was, "It's water over the deck—get over it." Easier said than done—if faced with a similar case in the future, the then-sitting justices will, no doubt, be mindful of the firestorm *Bush v. Gore* ignited, and it would not be surprising if, at that time, the Court looked for a way out, instead of a way in.

Whether *Bush v. Gore* will cause the American people to doubt the ostensibly apolitical nature of the Supreme Court in the future will likely depend on how the justices on the Court, especially the post-2000 appointees, acquit themselves in the public eye. If future decisions are perceived as exercises in which they strain to reach results that conform with their known predispositions, that will lead to one type of public perception, and comparisons to *Bush v. Gore* will be inevitable. If those decisions reflect objectivity and legal scholarship that lead to results that support no particular political or policy point of view, *Bush v. Gore* will likely be viewed as an historical anomaly, a one-time-only aberration with extreme political but limited precedential significance.

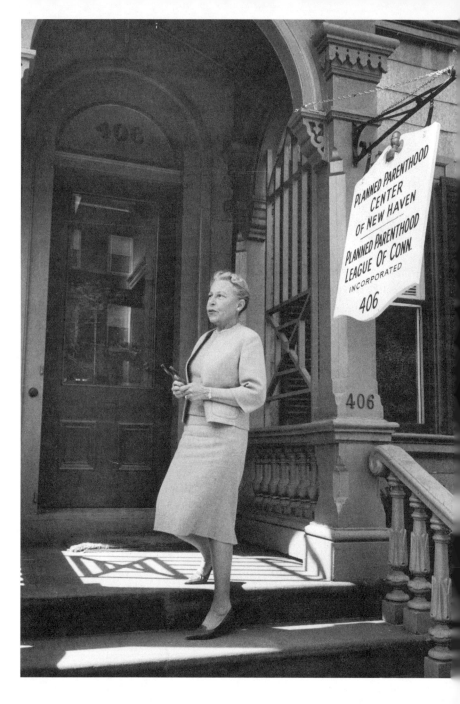

CHAPTER 6

THE RIGHT TO DO WHAT YOU WANT

*"The right to be let alone is indeed the
beginning of all freedom."*

—WILLIAM O. DOUGLAS,
SUPREME COURT JUSTICE, 1939–75

Justice Douglas was a staunch supporter of individual rights, but, as even he would concede, the yearning to be let alone must have its limits. As Justice Oliver Wendell Holmes Jr. put it, "The right to swing my fist ends where the other man's nose begins."

Still, Justice Holmes's commonsense rule creates its own conundrum: it is not always so easy to determine just where the other man's figurative nose really is.

Sometimes, of course, the line is obvious—you can't steal money or pollute a river. But what about when an individual minds his own business, but chooses to live his private life in a way that violates the majority's principles or sensibilities? Does the law have the right to tell you what you are allowed to do in your own house, or with your own body, or with your own family?

Estelle Griswold, executive director of Planned Parenthood, is pictured in front of the Connecticut center in April 1963; the center was closed pending decision of the U.S. Supreme Court in *Griswold v. Connecticut*.

16. Griswold v. Connecticut

The Unwritten Right of Privacy 1965

In *Griswold v. Connecticut*, the Supreme Court found within the Constitution a new and fundamental right: the right of privacy. In the process, the Supreme Court created the legal foundation on which, eight years later, *Roe v. Wade* was built, and on which other, as yet unforeseen, judicial results may also be founded. In addition, the *Griswold* case set off a conflagration, which continues through today, over the proper role of a Supreme Court justice in American society.

The background for the *Griswold* case goes back to 1879, when Connecticut passed a law outlawing contraception and making it a crime to use, or to assist or counsel anyone to use, "any drug, medicinal article or instrument for the purpose of preventing conception." The law was almost never enforced, but many persons found it an offensive intrusion into their personal lives, and wanted it off the books.

In the effort to create a test case to challenge the constitutionality of the law, Estelle Griswold, executive director of the Planned Parenthood League of Connecticut, and Dr. C. Lee Buxton, a physician and professor at the Yale School of Medicine, opened a birth-control clinic in New Haven. Shortly thereafter, they were arrested, tried, found guilty, and fined $100. They appealed, and the Supreme Court eventually agreed to hear their case.

Constitution or Conscience?

Sometimes a judge is presented with a case where justice and common sense cry out for a particular result, but there's no obvious law that allows the judge to get where he desperately wants to go. *Griswold* was that type of case. The vast majority of citizens, and all of the Supreme Court justices involved in *Griswold*, felt that the Connecticut law was an absurd and even repugnant invasion of the lives of married couples. Yet there was no apparent constitutional hook on which to hang the argument that the Connecticut statute was invalid.

Some justices, when faced with that kind of a case, view their sworn role as being limited to the enforcement of the Constitution as written, no matter the unfairness that may result in a particular situation. Their rationale is that if we are to remain a "government of laws and not men," some injustices may have to be suffered in order to avoid a greater evil—the creation of a judiciary in which justices are free to make up the law as they go along in order to dispense their own brands of situational equity.

Other justices, however, view their role much differently. They view the law in general, and the Constitution in particular, as a living, evolving rule book that has to change as society changes and as new, unforeseen situations are presented. They acknowledge an obligation to stay as close as feasible to the intent of the Constitution as written, but they view it as their duty to stretch its language in order to do what justice requires.

Penumbras and Emanations

Justice Douglas wrote the majority opinion in *Griswold*. He was an individualist who enthusiastically subscribed to the view that the law should be expanded when required to protect individual rights.

Justice Douglas conceded that the word "privacy" appears nowhere in the Constitution. Nevertheless, he concluded that, at least insofar as married couples are concerned, a fundamental right of privacy is implicit in the various guaranties given in the Bill of Rights, the first ten amendments to the Constitution. In some of the most famous (and ridiculed) language ever written by a Supreme Court justice, he offered that "specific guarantees in the Bill of Rights have penumbras, formed by emanations from those guarantees that help give them life and substance." For instance, the Fourth Amendment precludes unreasonable searches and seizures, which implies a right of privacy. The Fifth Amendment gives citizens the right against self-incrimination, which Justice Douglas likened to a personal "zone of privacy."

Two justices, Hugo Black and Potter Stewart, held judicial philosophies vastly different than Douglas's, and dissented. Justice Black found the Connecticut law "offensive." Justice Stewart called it "uncommonly silly." But that alone, they wrote, did not make it unconstitutional. Justice Black went on, "The Court talks about a constitutional 'right of privacy' as though there is some constitutional provision or provisions forbidding any law ever to be passed which might abridge the 'privacy' of individuals. But there is not." He concluded, "I like my privacy as well as the next one, but I am nevertheless compelled to admit that government has a right to invade it unless prohibited by some specific constitutional provision."

Griswold's Unintended Consequences

Griswold is extremely important, for at least two reasons: what the justices *said* in the case; and what the justices *did* in the case.

Concerning what was said in Griswold, by creating a new and fundamental right of privacy, Griswold provided a means for future Supreme Court justices to reach ends that were previously unreachable. The prime example is, of course, Roe v. Wade. In addition, however, Griswold was used as the legal justification for the Court to strike down laws barring the sale of contraceptives to unmarried couples in 1972; in 2003, in the case of Lawrence v. Texas, the Supreme Court, building on

Griswold without really admitting it, declared unconstitutional a state sodomy law and in the process invalidated all laws seeking to regulate intimate contact among adults.

Concerning what was done in *Griswold*, those who believe that the Constitution must be broadly interpreted to adjust to changing times were heartened, and those who believe that the Constitution must be strictly construed according to its language or, at most, the known intent of the framers, were outraged. Thanks in large part to *Griswold*, the judicial school of thought favored by a prospective justice has become a near-litmus test for those nominated to the Supreme Court. In their Senate confirmation hearings, prospective justices are routinely asked if they believe in a constitutional right to privacy. This is code for a question that asks, in one sense, if they would interpret the Constitution broadly or strictly and, in another sense, if they might consider reversing *Roe v. Wade*.

17. Roe v. Wade

Does the Right of Privacy Include the Right to an Abortion? 1973

Roe v. Wade is one of the most vigorously debated and politically sensitive Supreme Court decisions in American history. It arose out of a Texas statute that, like statutes in many other states, prohibited abortions except for the medical purpose of saving the mother's life. Roe, an unmarried pregnant woman who sought an abortion, filed a lawsuit in which she claimed the statute was unconstitutional, and the case was ultimately heard by the Supreme Court.

Roe won her case. Justice Harry Blackmun, joined by six other justices, ruled that the Constitution permits a woman to decide for herself whether to terminate her pregnancy, although the state could regulate abortion procedures in order to safeguard the woman's health and maintain medical standards. It is only when the fetus becomes able to live outside the womb, the Court ruled, that states may prohibit abortions, except those abortions required to preserve the life or health of the mother.

The fact that the justices were passionately at odds over *Roe*, and remain so, is well known. Justice Byron White, among others, wrote a withering dissent. "I find nothing in the language or history of the Constitution to support the Court's judgment . . . its judgment is an improvident and extravagant exercise of the power of judicial review that the Constitution extends to this Court." Justice Rehnquist wrote that the Roe majority based their decision on a supposed right that was "completely unknown" to the drafters of the Constitution.

In particular, two aspects of *Roe v. Wade* continue to stir wide-ranging fervor and controversy.

First, the Court refused to rule that, under the Constitution, an unborn child is a "person" entitled to constitutional protections. *Roe* is largely responsible for the raging political debate over when life begins, even though it failed to make a meaningful attempt to engage in the debate it created.

Second, the Court based much of its logic on a "right to privacy" that prior cases (like the *Griswold v. Connecticut* decision discussed earlier) found to exist within the Constitution, even though no such right is set forth in the Constitution in so many words. Using *Griswold* and similar cases as a legal stepping-stone, *Roe* expanded the newfound right to privacy "to encompass a woman's decision whether or not to terminate her pregnancy." Many commentators find the notion that the Constitution includes a fundamental right of privacy to be more fabrication than interpretation, and they further find the extension of that supposed right to abortion to be a logical and moral non sequitur. Others, of course, vehemently disagree.

Roe's Future, and the Future of Abortion

Despite the ongoing controversy, *Roe*'s central holding—that a woman has a right to an abortion up until the time the fetus is viable—has stood the test of time. The Court has struck down restrictions it deemed to unreasonably compromise the right to an abortion, such as state laws requiring a woman to obtain the consent of her husband. In 1992, in *Planned Parenthood v. Casey*, the Court reaffirmed its commitment to *Roe* and, while signaling that it would accept certain restrictions on the right to an abortion, it made plain that it would invalidate any restrictions that placed "an undue burden" on the right of a woman to obtain an abortion before the fetus attains viability.

The fate of *Roe* in either the long term or the short term is anything but certain. As the makeup of the Court changes, the odds for the reversal of *Roe* change as well. Whether *Roe*'s expansion of the constitutional right of privacy signals a trend, or comprises an aberration, may well depend on whether future presidents choose Supreme Court nominees who favor a strict or broad reading of the Constitution. This much is certain: abortion opponents will continue to test *Roe*, and the Supreme Court will have an ongoing flow of cases through which to expand, constrict, or reverse *Roe*.

But there is a common misconception that if *Roe* is reversed, abortion will be illegal. That's just not so. A ban on abortion would require a monumental shift in constitutional law, and perhaps a constitutional amendment.

Roe ruled that a state statute prohibiting abortion is unconstitutional; if *Roe* is reversed, states will be permitted, as they were before *Roe*, to outlaw abortion—but states will also have the right, as they did before *Roe*, *not* to outlaw abortion. The upshot will likely be a political maelstrom of activity in state legislatures across the country, including a variety of ballot initiatives and referenda, all of which will lead to a regulatory crazy quilt in which some states allow abortion and other states prohibit it.

Still, for some women, the reversal of *Roe* could, as a practical matter, eliminate their ability to obtain an abortion: if they live in a state where abortion is illegal, health or financial constraints may make it impossible for them to travel to another state, particularly if adjoining states enact lengthy residency requirements as a way to avoid becoming abortion havens.

The debate specifically over *Roe* is not, therefore, a debate over whether abortion should be legal or illegal, as much as it is a debate over whether the ability to obtain an abortion should be made easier or more difficult, or should be made to depend on a woman's financial circumstances, or should be made to depend on geography.

18. Washington v. Glucksberg

The Right to Die 1997

Suppose a close friend becomes terminally ill, all quality of life has evaporated, and he is suffering. Moreover, his medical bills will dissipate his assets, and he is desperately worried about his family's financial future. He tells you he would prefer to die—peacefully, without pain, now. He pleads with you, as his closest friend, to help him carry out his wishes. All you need to do is fill an old painkiller prescription he has, give him the bottle, and he will do the rest. May you do it? May you arrange for a doctor or nurse to help him, and even if you could, would they be permitted to do anything?

As of this writing, forty-nine states prohibit assisted suicide, and in recent years doctors, terminally ill patients, and "death with dignity" organizations have challenged the constitutionality of these laws in court. One such challenge was mounted in the mid-1990s by Dr. Harold Glucksberg, along with other physicians, patients, and a nonprofit advocacy group. It involved a Washington state statute that makes "promoting a suicide" a felony. Glucksberg sought the right to honor the wishes of terminal patients who asked for his assistance. The case, *Washington v. Glucksberg*, made its way to the Supreme Court in 1997.

The Limits of Liberty

Glucksberg, like most litigants who have challenged assisted-suicide bans, based his case on the historic Due Process Clause of the Fourteenth Amendment, which prohibits a state from depriving persons of "life, liberty, or property without due process of law." Surely, Glucksberg contended, this constitutional right of liberty must include the right of a competent adult to choose to die, and to seek assistance in implementing that decision. As the saying goes, it's a free country.

Some lower courts had agreed with this argument in other cases, but the Supreme Court, in an opinion written by Chief Justice Rehnquist, unanimously disagreed. The Court found that the Due Process Clause does not prevent government from regulating all conceivable liberties, but only certain fundamental liberties rooted in the nation's history and traditions. The Court reviewed Anglo-American law since the 1400s, and found that England, and then the colonies, had prohibited assisted suicides for hundreds of years. Therefore, the Court ruled, there was no reason to believe that the framers of the Constitution intended to contravene this tradition and establish a "right to die." Consequently, said the Court, it was not unconstitutional for a state to criminalize assisted suicide.

Keep in mind, however, that while *Washington v. Glucksberg* stands for the proposition that states may lawfully prohibit assisted suicides within their borders, states may, conversely, allow assisted suicides if they wish. So far, Oregon is the only state to have done so, enacting the Death with Dignity Act, which became effective in 1997. The law permits physicians, in well-defined circumstances, to provide a lethal dosage of pills to terminally ill patients who seek to end their own suffering. It is then up to the patient to take the pills, or not. The Bush administration challenged the constitutionality of the Death with Dignity Act and, in January 2006, the Supreme Court, while not endorsing the law, refused to overturn it, in a 6–3 vote. Several other states were awaiting the outcome of this ruling, and will now likely introduce similar legislation.

As was the case with abortion before *Roe v. Wade* (and as will be the case if *Roe* is overruled), whether or not you have the right to die through assisted suicide will, for the foreseeable future, depend on where you live.

19. District of Columbia v. Heller

The Right to Bear Arms 2008

Does the right to do what you want include the right to carry a handgun? Consider the arcane language of the Second Amendment: "A well regulated Militia, being necessary to the security of a free State, the right of the people to keep and bear Arms, shall not be infringed."

The Supreme Court's job is to determine what the Constitution means. Typically, that entails taking an understandable phrase and figuring out how it applies to a specific situation. For example, does criminalizing flag burning violate the First Amendment's prohibition against "abridging the freedom of speech"? Or does the practice of using a high-tech device placed outside a house to detect what might be going on inside violate the Fourth Amendment's prohibition against "unreasonable searches"? Or does the Constitution's guaranty of "equal protection" permit "separate but equal" treatment?

These are difficult, often tortuous issues. But in approaching these questions, the Supreme Court is at least dealing with comprehensible phraseology. We have a basic, shared understanding of the meaning of phrases like "abridging the freedom of speech," "unreasonable searches," and "equal protection." Individual justices may disagree on how to apply the words chosen by the framers of the Constitution to the circumstances of particular cases that come before the Court. But at least the justices start out on the same page, talking about basically the same generally understood concepts.

Not so with the Second Amendment, where, for decades, justices have disagreed over its basic meaning, as if they were debating the proper translation of an ancient text. The dispute centers on how the two clauses fit together. The first clause says that we need a "well regulated Militia." The second speaks of "the right of the people to keep and bear Arms." Does the first clause govern the second clause, such that the framers only intended to provide that the government cannot disarm citizens who are part of organized militias? Given the historical context, that interpretation makes sense. Just a few years earlier, groups of citizens formed their own militias, armed themselves with their own weapons, and helped to free the colonies from English rule. The framers most certainly understood that the best defense against a tyrannical government was an armed militia, and they would have wanted to prevent the new government from disarming the citizens who might find it necessary to join such militias in the future.

Or is the first clause just one example of why the right of the people to bear arms was so important to the framers? If the right were meant only to apply to people who served in militias, wouldn't the framers (classically educated men who most certainly knew how to express themselves) have said so? The second clause plainly references the right of *the people* to keep and bear Arms—not just the right of the people who serve in militias.

People often see what they want to see in the Second Amendment. Gun-control advocates argue that the first clause takes precedence, and that the Second Amendment grants only a militia-based, collective right to bear arms. Gun-rights advocates argue that the reference to "the people" in the second clause means just what it says, and that the Second Amendment grants each individual, whether or not connected to a militia, the right to bear arms. It is among our most hot-button issues. In many parts of the country, a candidate's stance on the Second Amendment will determine an election.

In 2008, the Supreme Court decided to reopen the question.

The Making of a Test Case

Heller was a classic test case, carefully constructed by organized and well-funded gun-rights advocates to focus on a narrow question: does the Second Amendment provide an individual who is not affiliated with a militia the right to keep a gun in his home for purposes of self-defense? Their interest was in establishing that the Second Amendment was an *individual* right, not just the collective right of those in military service. Everything else having to do with what that right meant, how it might be limited, and in what other contexts it applied would await another day in court.

To raise that pristine question, they focused on the District of Columbia's gun ban, the nation's most extreme. The District had earned the unfortunate designation as the "murder capital of America," with the highest rate of firearms deaths per capita in the United States. In the hope of limiting the proliferation of firearms, the District effectively outlawed all handguns from homes, and required that rifles and shotguns could only be kept in homes if they were unloaded, disassembled, and bound by a trigger lock.

Those promoting the test case chose a group of citizens with diverse backgrounds to challenge the ban. For arcane legal reasons, only one, Dick Heller, remained to carry the issue by the time the case made it to the Supreme Court. Heller, a security guard with a spotless background who lived in the District, had tried to register a handgun that he wished to keep in his home for self-defense. Based solely on the District's gun ban, he was turned down.

Heller's position was simple. It removed all of the nuance and complexity, and framed the issue in a way the Supreme Court could not avoid. There was no question that Heller lived in an area where self-defense is a real concern. There was nothing about Heller himself that would justify denying him a handgun to be used for self-defense. All he asked for was the right to keep the kind of handgun in his home that is commonly used for self-defense. He raised no issue about his right to keep other kinds of guns, or to carry a gun outside of his home. The District's law gave him no other viable self-defense option—he could keep a rifle or shotgun in his home, but an armed intruder would not be likely to wait while he reassembled it and took off the trigger lock.

If, Heller argued to the Supreme Court, the Second Amendment gives individuals a constitutional right to own guns, then I have to win—I need a gun in my home for self-defense, I'm a sane and law-abiding adult, and there's no rational reason for the government to stop me. So just answer that one question for me, yes or no: does the Second Amendment give me that right, or not?

Ideological Conservatives v. Ideological Liberals

The Court answered the question, and in doing so it split 5–4, along predictable, ideological lines—the Second Amendment retained its mirror-like ability to reflect what those who read it hope it says.

The so-called conservative wing of the Court (Justices Scalia, Thomas, Kennedy, Roberts, and Alito) won the day, and took the politically conservative position. Justice Antonin Scalia wrote the majority opinion, ultimately concluding that the right to bear arms is each individual's right, having nothing to do with service in a militia. "In sum," he wrote, "we hold that the District's ban on handgun possession in the home violates the Second Amendment, as does its prohibition against rendering any lawful firearm in the home operable for the purpose of immediate self-defense."

To reach that conclusion, Justice Scalia looked at the historical context in which the framers of the Constitution drafted the Second Amendment. The framers often used the term "the people," he reasoned, and when they did so they meant *all* the people, not just some subset, such as those who happened to be in militias. In the eighteenth century, unlike today, the militia *was* "the people," and the initial clause was not meant as a limitation on the right to bear arms. "Does the preface fit with an operative clause that creates an individual right to keep and bear arms?" Scalia asked. "It fits perfectly." Therefore, he ruled, the Second Amendment "surely elevates above all other interests the right of law-abiding, responsible citizens to use arms in defense of hearth and home." Gun possession may cause problems, he reasoned, but we cannot solve those problems through the violation of fundamental constitutional rights.

The so-called liberal wing of the Court (Justices Stevens, Souter, Ginsburg, and Breyer) took the politically liberal position, and dissented. Justice John Paul Stevens wrote one of the dissents and, like Justice Scalia, he analyzed the historical context—and reached the opposite conclusion. He called Justice Scalia's interpretation of history "strained and unpersuasive." Justice Stevens argued that in addition to the focus on militias in the first clause, the phrase "to keep and bear arms" in the second clause was the kind of language that, at the time, pertained to military-like service. "The Court would have us believe that over 200 years ago, the Framers made a choice to limit the tools available to elected officials wishing to regulate civilian uses of weapons," he wrote. "I could not possibly conclude that the Framers made such a choice."

Typically, so-called conservatives respect precedent, and criticize so-called liberals as being "activists" who too easily upset settled law to serve their own agendas. Here, Justice Stevens argued, it was the conservatives who were guilty of those judicial sins. "Until today, it has been understood that legislatures may regulate the civilian use and misuse of firearms so long as they do not interfere with the preservation of a well-regulated militia," Justice Stevens wrote in his dissent. "The

Court's announcement of a new constitutional right to own and use firearms for private purposes upsets that settled understanding."

So Much for Gun Bans. What about Gun Controls?

Most modern constitutional scholars, even those who might call themselves political "liberals," seem to agree that despite its awkward syntax, the Second Amendment *was* meant to provide an individual right to bear arms, not just a collective right to do so within a militia. President Obama, for instance, a longtime constitutional law professor, agrees with this conclusion.

The real disagreement, however, centers on the issue of how far a town, a state, or the Congress can go in regulating that right.

Justice Stephen Breyer wrote a dissent in *Heller* in which he argued that even if there is an individual right to own a gun, it's not the same sort of right as free speech or freedom of religion. The law should allow an "interest-balancing approach" when it comes to firearms, he reasoned. We regulate all kinds of rights based on public safety (even free speech, as in the clichéd prohibition against yelling "Fire!" in a public theater), and if, as in the District of Columbia, there is a truly compelling need to ban firearms, the Second Amendment's right to bear arms should yield.

All of the liberals, and none of the conservatives, signed on to Justice Breyer's view. The conservatives saw the Second Amendment as something much more sacrosanct than Justice Breyer's view implied.

But at the same time, Justice Scalia's majority opinion made clear that *some* forms of gun control regulation *would* be permissible. Yes, the Second Amendment provides a right to bear arms, Justice Scalia wrote, but it is "not a right to keep and carry any weapon whatsoever in any manner whatsoever and for whatever purpose." He took pains to point out that the decision "should [not] be taken to cast doubt" on the many forms of existing gun regulation. As Justice Stevens noted in his dissent, the *Heller* decision "leaves for future cases the formidable task of defining the scope" of future regulation on the right to bear arms.

In all likelihood, the *Heller* decision will leave unscathed basic firearm licensing laws, certain limits on commercial sales, bans on possession of firearms by felons and mentally ill persons, and bans on gun possession in certain areas such as near schools and government buildings. It will also allow bans on certain "dangerous and unusual" weapons. But the parameters of these controls remain unknown. "Since this case represents this Court's first in-depth examination of the Second Amendment," Justice Scalia wrote, "one should not expect it to clarify the entire field."

These issues will be decided by future courts in future cases, through the same exquisite ballet that has shaped our right of free speech, our religious rights, our rights to be free from unreasonable searches, our rights of equal protection and due process, and all of the other rights that define so much of America. Court challenges to existing and newly formulated regulations will be filed; lower courts will make decisions; the Supreme Court will review some of those decisions; and new lines will be drawn. The ultimate result will depend on the predilections of those who sit on the Supreme Court in the future, a topic discused in the final chapter. In the meantime, there will be uncertainty, which is one of the prices to be paid in a democracy where, thankfully, the law evolves through a participatory and deliberative—often political—process. Not perfect, but consider the alternatives.

Thirty-ninth Congress of the United States, at the first Session, begun and held at the City of Washington, in the District of Columbia, on Monday the fourth day of December, one thousand eight hundred and sixty-five.

Joint Resolution proposing an amendment to the Constitution of the United States.

Be it resolved by the Senate and House of Representatives of the United States of America in Congress assembled, (two-thirds of both Houses concurring,) That the following article be proposed to the legislatures of the several States as an amendment to the Constitution of the United States, which, when ratified by three-fourths of said legislatures, shall be valid as part of the Constitution, namely:

Article XIV.

Section 1. All persons born or naturalized in the United States, and subject to the jurisdiction thereof, are citizens of the United States and of the State therein they reside. No State shall make or enforce any law which shall abridge the privileges or immunities of citizens of the United States; nor shall any State deprive any person of life, liberty, or property, without due process of law; nor deny to any person within its jurisdiction the equal protection of the laws.

Section 2. Representatives shall be apportioned among the several States according to their respective numbers, counting the whole number of persons in each State, excluding Indians not taxed. But when the right to vote at any election for the choice of electors for President and Vice President of the United States, Representatives in Congress, the Executive and Judicial officers of a State, or the members of the Legislature thereof, is denied to any of the male inhabitants of such State, being twenty-one years of age, and citizens of the United States, or in any way abridged, except for participation in rebellion, or other crime, the basis of representation therein shall be reduced in the proportion which the

CHAPTER 7

"BIG GOVERNMENT" IN YOUR BUSINESS AND YOUR BACKYARD

*"Liberty implies the absence of arbitrary restraint,
not immunity from reasonable regulations . . ."*

— JUSTICE CHARLES EVANS HUGHES

The venerated Due Process Clause of the Fourteenth Amendment prohibits the government from depriving any person "of life, liberty, or property, without due process of law." Stated differently, the government *can* take your property, your liberty, and even your life, so long as it goes about doing it in the right way.

This principle applies in a myriad of contexts, one of which is the world of commerce: just how far can the government go in restricting how people conduct business, or in regulating what happens on the job, or in deciding who wins the conflicts between business interests and individual rights?

The answer to these questions can be complex, implicating not only the Due Process Clause, but other constitutional provisions as well. Decades ago, the Supreme Court seemingly defined much of this legal landscape but, as will be seen, it may now be in the process of changing its mind in important ways, and where it ultimately ends up will have profound effects on the role of government in our society.

A detail of page one of the Fourteenth Amendment.

20. West Coast Hotel Co. v. Parrish

What Gives Congress the Right to Regulate
Private Businesses? 1937

In the early 1900s, state legislatures began to enact measures designed to protect workers, such as child labor laws, maximum hour laws, and workers compensation laws. The Supreme Court, however, quickly put the constitutional brakes on these efforts, setting the stage for a momentous power struggle and constitutional crisis decades later. The outcome of that struggle would determine not only whether Congress would be permitted to protect workers, but also whether it would be permitted to address the country's social issues, ranging from outlawing segregation to protecting the food supply.

The conflict began in earnest when New York enacted a law limiting the work week to a maximum of sixty hours in certain industries. The law was challenged, and in 1905 the case, *Lochner v. New York*, worked its way to the Supreme Court. The Court's analysis in *Lochner* focused on the Due Process Clause of the Fourteenth Amendment to the Constitution: "No person shall be . . . deprived of life, liberty, or property, without due process of law." Central to this right, said the Court, was the liberty to enter into contracts without government interference, and that included contracts between employers and employees. Based on that logic, in a 5–4 decision the Court ruled that laws "limiting the hours in which grown and intelligent men may labor to earn their living" are "mere meddlesome interferences with the rights of the individual." The New York law was ruled unconstitutional. In effect, the Supreme Court ruled that the government was obligated to leave businesses, and the people who worked for and dealt with businesses, to their own devices.

Roosevelt's Reaction: The "Court-Packing Plan"

Lochner remained unchallenged until Franklin D. Roosevelt and the "New Dealers" took power in the wake of the Great Depression. A fundamental part of Roosevelt's economic recovery plan was the implementation of health and safety codes. Court challenges to these codes predictably resulted, and in 1935, using the *Lochner* precedent, the Supreme Court began to dismantle what Roosevelt had done: it invalidated an act that allowed farmers to hold on to their farms during foreclosure; it invalidated minimum wage, maximum hour, and health codes in the poultry industry; and it invalidated Roosevelt's key agricultural reforms.

Roosevelt was beyond livid, and on February 5, 1937, he unveiled what came to be known as the "court-packing plan": Roosevelt sought to cajole Congress into passing a law that would allow him to appoint an extra Supreme Court justice for each present justice who was over seventy, which, at that time, would have increased the number of justices from nine to sixteen. Roosevelt's ostensible purpose was to assist older justices to carry the Court's workload, but his obvious intent was to gain control over a Court that he viewed as a dangerous impediment to economic recovery and social justice. Roosevelt lobbied hard for the legislation through vituperative attacks on the Court, back-room deal-making, and nationally broadcast "fireside chats." While there was support for the plan in some quarters, there was substantial suspicion as well—if the president could, essentially, "rig" the Court to suit his purposes, what would become of the "check and balance" role the Supreme Court was to play in the Constitution's elegant plan?

Less than two months later, while Senate hearings on Roosevelt's plan were proceeding, the Supreme Court handed down a decision in the case of *West Coast Hotel Co. v. Parrish*. The case involved a challenge to the constitutionality of the state of Washington's minimum wage laws. The Supreme Court had recently overturned similar laws by a 5–4 margin, and it was expected that the *West Coast Hotel* case would face the same fate.

The Switch in Time That Saved Nine

This time, however, the 5–4 majority went the other way—one of the justices, Justice Owen J. Roberts, inexplicably switched his vote and signed on to an opinion authored by Chief Justice Charles Evans Hughes, who abandoned *Lochner* in favor of a rationale that became the foundation for national minimum-wage laws, Social Security, the regulation of public utilities, agricultural quotas, and much more. Liberty, said the chief justice (along with his newfound colleague), be it freedom of contract or any other liberty, is not absolute, but can and must be regulated so that the citizenry may be protected against "the evils which menace the health, safety, morals, and welfare of the people."

This was sweet music to FDR's ears, and the confrontation between the executive and the judiciary quickly became a collaboration. Justice Roberts's change of heart was soon dubbed the "switch in time that saved nine." Historians have never been able to definitively establish whether Justice Roberts's turnabout was the result of the pressure exerted by Roosevelt on the Court, or an honest change in viewpoint but, in the years that followed, Roosevelt was able to implement the social legislation of the New Deal without further interference from the Supreme Court, and the congressional impetus to keep enacting such legislation continued for more than fifty years.

21. Heart of Atlanta Motel v. United States
22. Katzenbach v. McClung

What Are the Limits on Congress's Right to Regulate Business, and Beyond? 1964

The *West Coast Hotel* case cleared the way for Congress, whether on its own or at the urging of the president, to enact broad-brush business legislation that changed the way Americans live. But the decision raised two far-reaching questions.

First, does the federal government's right to regulate business stop at the national or, at worst, the industry level? Or can it also reach into local communities and regulate individual businesses? For instance, can the federal government dictate how much the corner store must pay its employees, or what hours it can operate? Or should issues like those be decided strictly on the community or, at worst, the state level?

Second, if the federal government is ultimately allowed to reach into local towns in order to tell businesses how to behave, is it also allowed to dictate what subjects must be taught in the local schools, and who the local police department is permitted to hire? Where does the power stop?

Much of the answer lies in a provision in the Constitution known as the "Commerce Clause," and the extent of the power that provision gives the federal government is now the subject of one of the hottest Supreme Court debates in decades. Two cases decided in the 1960s, *Heart of Atlanta Motel v. United States* and *Katzenbach v. McClung*, took the pendulum about as far as it could go in one direction, but it now appears to be quickly swinging the other way.

Some background is necessary to understand how we got where we are, and where we may be going.

The Supreme Court Expands the Commerce Clause

In the years before the Constitution was created, the states had been waging economic wars among themselves through protective tariffs and retaliatory trade regulations, making the creation of a national economy virtually impossible. This was one of the major reasons why the Founding Fathers convened a Constitutional Convention—the goal was to forge a federal government with sufficient power to create a workable system of national commerce. The so-called Commerce Clause of the Constitution was the result: it granted Congress the power "to Regulate Commerce with foreign nations, and among the Several States, and with the Indian Tribes."

In the early nineteenth century, Congress began to flex its federal muscles, and it enacted a variety of laws requiring that the states cease interference with interstate commerce so that a national economy might develop more quickly. For instance, it imposed interstate rail and shipping rates and practices so that one state could not, through its own laws, obtain an economic leg up on another state. When these laws were challenged as being beyond congressional authority, the Supreme Court ruled that, in fact, Congress had been empowered by the Commerce Clause to regulate interstate commerce, and it therefore had the right under the Constitution to take such actions.

Through the remainder of the nineteenth century and into the twentieth century, as industry expanded and the economy grew, Congress further amplified its legislative activities, and the businesses that bore the brunt of these regulations again challenged them in court. Often, the challenge was based on the fact that the activity Congress sought to regulate took place within just one state, as opposed to taking place in "interstate commerce." For instance, Congress passed laws regulating what occurred in stockyards, even though each stockyard was situated in only a single state.

The Supreme Court allowed these laws to stand, by dramatically expanding the concept of "interstate commerce" to include economic activities that took place solely within one state, on the theory that such activities plainly affected commerce in other states. For example, it ruled that a stockyard located and doing business only in Chicago could nonetheless be regulated by Congress because the livestock in the stockyard were ultimately destined for shipment to states all over the country—that is, the stockyard was connected to an interstate distribution chain and was therefore itself in interstate commerce. Using this interpretation of "interstate commerce," the Court allowed Congress to implement legislation imposing workplace rules, establishing union rights, mandating payment for overtime, setting commodity prices, regulating strip mining, and controlling a host of other in-state economic activities, all on the theory that the activities "affected" interstate commerce, and were therefore authorized by the Commerce Clause.

Taking the Commerce Clause to, and Perhaps Beyond, the Limit

The Supreme Court's willingness to expand Congress's rights under the Commerce Clause reached a zenith in 1964. Congress passed the Civil Rights Act of 1964 to prohibit discrimination on the basis of race, color, religion, or national origin in places of public accommodation, like hotels and restaurants. Congress knew that its right to regulate private conduct of this type was questionable—the Civil Rights Act did not really focus on regulating economic activity in the same way that legislation affecting, for instance, stockyards and commodities did. It was plainly focused on ending discrimination, and nothing more. However, Congress inserted a provision stating that a facility was covered under the Act "if its operations affect commerce," Congress hoped that the Supreme Court would use that language as a hook to rule that the Commerce Clause gave Congress the power it needed to do just about anything Congress wanted to do.

As expected, the Civil Rights Act of 1964 was immediately challenged in court. The Heart of Atlanta Motel, located in downtown Atlanta, insisted on continuing its practice of refusing to rent rooms to blacks. The motel was near a highway and served intrastate as well as interstate travelers. Similarly, Ollie's Barbecue, a large restaurant in Birmingham, Alabama, insisted on continuing its practice of serving whites at tables, but providing only takeout service for blacks. It purchased some of its food—approximately $70,000 a year—from out-of-state suppliers, and served interstate travelers. The owners of both establishments argued that the Commerce Clause could not logically be used to give the federal government regulatory power over their businesses, which had only microscopic and indirect effects on interstate commerce.

The cases that resulted from these court challenges, *Heart of Atlanta Motel v. United States and Katzenbach v. McClung,* ultimately reached the Supreme Court—and in deciding those cases, the Court upheld the power of Congress to enact the Civil Rights Act of 1964 pursuant to the authority granted by the Commerce Clause. These decisions were monumentally important: for better or worse, they validated Congress's right not only to fight racial discrimination throughout the country, but to reach into local towns and attack virtually all manner of social ills and wrongs through federal lawmaking. The body of social legislation that arose from Congress during the 1960s, 1970s, and 1980s can in large measure be attributed to these decisions.

The rationale the Court used in the *Heart of Atlanta Motel* and *Katzenbach* cases stretched the words of the Commerce Clause to (and some say beyond) their limits. The Court reasoned that both businesses, even though they did not directly engage in interstate commerce, catered to people who themselves moved in interstate commerce, and it stood to reason that the cumulative effect of discriminating against a portion of those people affected interstate commerce in some substantial way. It was not necessary, said the Court, to engage in quantification efforts or detailed analyses—if it could be rationally concluded that the activities Congress was regulating had a material effect on interstate commerce, that was enough.

The Supreme Court's Retreat

Based on these Commerce Clause precedents, there was little that was beyond Congress's reach—and Congress took full advantage of its power, enacting federal legislation that affected innumerable aspects of local life. Critics complained that this distorted the Commerce Clause beyond its plain meaning and gave Congress powers the Founding Fathers had never intended it to have.

By 1995, however, a majority of the Supreme Court was comprised of justices who shared these critics' judicial philosophies, and the result has been a serious change in direction, with major implications.

It began with the 1995 case of *United States v. Lopez*. The Supreme Court addressed the constitutionality of the Gun-Free School Zones Act of 1990, in which Congress made it a federal offense for a person to possess a firearm in a school zone. The Act was challenged in court, and, in a 5–4 decision handed down in 1995, the Supreme Court ruled that the regulation of guns in school zones did not involve a sufficient connection to economic activity to implicate the federal government's Commerce

Clause powers, and the federal government was therefore legislating in a realm in which it had no authority. The decision floored most legal analysts, who had come to take the Commerce Clause for granted.

Five years later, in 2000, the Supreme Court did it again. In the case of *United States v. Morrison*, the Court faced a challenge to a federal law that prohibited violence against women. In another 5–4 decision, the Supreme Court ruled that the law exceeded the federal government's power under the Commerce Clause. Even though violence against women may have economic implications that affect interstate commerce, the Court ruled that "crimes of violence are not, in any sense of the phrase, economic activity" and Congress was therefore not empowered under the Commerce Clause to legislate in that arena. *Lopez* was no longer an aberration; it appeared to be part of a trend.

In both cases, the four dissenting justices fervently pointed out that Congress had assembled evidence in reports and hearings establishing that violence in schools substantially affects the quality of education, and a lesser-educated workforce has an obvious affect on interstate commerce. Even more troubling, they reasoned, Congress had established a "mountain of data" assembled during four years of hearings documenting the substantial effects that violence against women has on the economy—far more than any evidence that supported the decisions in the *Heart of Atlanta Motel* and *Katzenbach* cases. The majority was unmoved.

These cases, and the whole idea of the Commerce Clause, may seem somewhat esoteric, but they raise a fundamental issue: what is the role of the federal government in solving the country's social problems? The law is plainly in flux, but the current Court may be bent on transferring a substantial degree of responsibility for social problems from the Capitol to the statehouses and the town halls.

23. Burlington Industries v. Ellerth

Expanding the Right of Employees to Sue Their Employers 1998

Sometimes it is the Supreme Court itself, not Congress, that multiplies the scope and effect of government regulation. Such was the case in the 1998 case of *Burlington Industries v. Ellerth*, where the Supreme Court, acting in the role of interpreting an Act of Congress, changed the rules of the American workplace, and made it much easier for employees to win sexual-harassment and other lawsuits against their employers. The result has been a major increase in employee versus employer lawsuits, many ending in six- and seven-figure verdicts, and a radical shift in the way employers must manage their workforces.

Ellerth, a Burlington Industries salesperson, was subjected to constant sexual harassment from her supervisor. However, even though she knew that Burlington prohibited sexual harassment, she did not report her supervisor's misconduct, and she eventually quit. Ellerth then sued Burlington, claiming that the sexual harassment forced her to resign.

At the trial, Burlington proved that it had done all anyone could have reasonably expected it to do. It had established clear policies forbidding sexual harassment; it did not know about the sexual harassment that Ellerth had suffered; and, absent a report from Ellerth, it had no realistic way of finding out about it. Burlington's defense was airtight: it was not negligent, and, as a result, it should not he held liable for the unknown acts of a renegade supervisor who was furtively violating Burlington's policies. Burlington won the case in the trial court.

Ellerth filed an appeal, and ultimately the Supreme Court agreed to hear her case. Ellerth contended that the Supreme Court should change the law of sexual harassment by applying a legal doctrine well entrenched in other kinds of cases, known as "vicarious liability." If, for instance, a company's truck driver runs a red light and causes an accident, the law provides that the company is "vicariously liable" for the actions of its employee, whether or not the company was itself negligent. The same would be true if, for instance, a nurse working for a group of doctors negligently injured a patient, or if a waiter working for a restaurant dropped a tray on a customer. In each case, the employer would be vicariously liable for the actions of its employee, even though the employer itself had done nothing wrong.

Why, asked Ellerth, shouldn't Burlington be vicariously liable for what its supervisor did to her, even if Burlington itself was not directly at fault?

Ellerth won—with some complications. The *Ellerth* case boiled down to two crucial rulings, each of which comprises a sea change in the law of the workplace.

First, the Supreme Court ruled that in cases where a supervisor sexually harasses an employee, and in the process takes some negative action against the employee (such as denying a raise or promotion), the company will be held liable, no matter what, even if the company actively prohibited sexual harassment, never knew that the sexual harassment was taking place, and did nothing else wrong.

Second, the Supreme Court ruled that even when no negative action is taken against the employee, if the employee is made to work in a sexually suggestive atmosphere that is unreasonably offensive—what the courts call a "hostile work environment"—the employer will be held liable, unless it can prove that it did all it reasonably could to prevent and correct the harassment and that the employee failed to take advantage of preventive or corrective opportunities the employer provided.

The Workplace, Reworked

Since the *Ellerth* decision was rendered, its directives has been expanded beyond the sexual harassment context and into related areas such as, for instance, employee allegations of harassment or discrimination based on race, nationality and religion. Old rule: an employer is not liable for a supervisor's unlawful treatment of an employee unless the employer is at fault by, for instance, knowingly permitting a renegade supervisor to remain on the job. New rule: employers must *proactively* train and police their supervisors as part of a program to prevent unlawful conduct *before* it happens and must aggressively address *all* allegations of unlawful conduct as soon as they surface—if they do not, they risk an avalanche of lawsuits to which they may have no defense.

The upshot of *Ellerth* has been a massive shift in the balance of power between employees and their employers. As so often happens, this change in legal fundamentals fomented a change in societal fundamentals. The amplified risk of employee claims created, as a matter of financial necessity, the need for employers to mandate new standards of conduct not only between management and employees, but among employees themselves.

After only a decade (the blink of an eye in legal terms), *Ellerth's* transformation of the employer-employee rules of engagement has markedly changed the interactions and economics of the American workplace.

24. Standard Oil Co. v. United States

Eliminating Monopolies and Price-Fixing:
John D. Rockefeller and the Birth of the Antitrust Laws 1911

Think what things would be like if there were only one or two cell-phone providers, pharmaceutical firms, or automobile companies. As things stand, you cannot watch television or read a magazine without being deluged with advertisements touting the superiority of one brand over another, and the price wars among competing companies can be fierce. But if there were only one or two companies in these fields, the incentive to innovate new and better products at cheaper prices would not be nearly as intense—and the consumer would suffer. Competition has always been viewed as a key to the free enterprise system.

"Antitrust law" is designed to preserve competition. The basic statutes were enacted by Congress in the late 1800s and early 1900s, but it was the Supreme Court that put flesh on the statutory bones, beginning in 1911 with the *Standard Oil Co. v. United States* case.

Restraints of Trade and the "Rule of Reason"

The Standard Oil Company was founded by John D. Rockefeller. Through a combination of ruthlessness and creativity, Rockefeller managed to combine the vast majority of the country's oil refining and distribution capacities under one roof, creating a classic monopoly. Having eliminated the competition, he could sell and charge what he wanted to whomever he wanted, and he did.

Spurred by muckraking journalists, the government ultimately took action and brought suit, under the relatively new Sherman Antitrust Act, to break up Standard Oil into separate, competitive businesses.

The trial consumed weeks (the record includes some 14,000 pages of testimony), and the Supreme Court eventually agreed to render the final ruling.

In an undeniably landmark case, the Court broke up Standard Oil into separate, geographic units (not unlike what happened in the telephone industry decades later). In so doing, the Court announced a new rule to be applied in future monopoly cases—the so-called "rule of reason." The Sherman Act had prohibited any "restraint of trade," but the Supreme Court decided that only "unreasonable" restraints of trade (of which Standard Oil was the poster child) would be unlawful. In so doing, the Supreme Court gave birth to the federal government's power to analyze and, if warranted, seek the breakup of companies (as it attempted to do to Microsoft) and to minutely review and, if warranted, disallow proposed mergers that might restrain competition.

Price Fixing and "Per Se" Violations

Ever creative, companies in the early 1900s pursued another activity that allowed them to raise prices without creating monopolies: price fixing agreements. The leaders of competing companies in an industry would simply agree among themselves to maintain prices at an agreed-upon level, rather than trying to undercut one another. The usual effects of competition would be blunted, and the consumer would suffer.

Building on the *Standard Oil* precedent, in 1927, in the case of *United States v. Trenton Potteries Co.*, the Supreme Court ruled that price fixing agreements among competitors are by definition an unreasonable restraint of trade, whether or not the levels at which prices were fixed were or were not reasonable. This became known as a "per se" violation of the antitrust laws, meaning that simply doing it is against the law, without regard for any "rule of reason." In the intervening decades, various other forms of collusion among ostensible competitors have been identified as per se violations as well.

Antitrust law has evolved into a huge body of court decisions, statutes, and regulations that permit both enforcement actions by the government and suits by private citizens and companies for antitrust violations. Scholarly debates among economists and politicians pertaining to the economic policies that should underlie the enforcement of the antitrust laws are ongoing, leading to different approaches taken by different administrations and different courts at different times. But when all is said and done, in the *Standard Oil* case the Supreme Court set forth the basics of some of the most important rules by which corporate America must live.

25. Kelo v. City of New London

Can the Government Take Your House to
Promote a Private Business? 2005

The concept of the government taking your house because it wants to use your property for some other purpose is frightening to contemplate. However, even before the Constitution was drafted in 1787, it was a given that a sovereign nation had this power of "eminent domain" or "condemnation." Our Founding Fathers recognized this in the Fifth Amendment to the Constitution, but restricted the right of the government to take private property (upon payment of just compensation) to one purpose: "public use."

Most citizens understand this as a necessary but limited evil that allows the government to take private property only in very rare circumstances, such as when a house lies in the path of a needed highway that will be used by the general public, or for a water-treatment plant or similar public facility. Taking someone's home is not something a democracy that respects individual rights does unless absolutely necessary.

But can private property be lawfully taken in order to promote private business interests?

A Castle No More?

In 1997, Susette Kelo purchased and restored a home with a river view in the Fort Trumbull neighborhood in New London, Connecticut. Many other families lived in this older, middle-class neighborhood as well; some had been there for many generations.

New London's economy had been faltering for some time and, in 1998, the pharmaceutical company Pfizer began building a major research facility next to the Fort Trumbull neighborhood. New London saw this as an opportunity for economic development and revitalization and, through a private development agency controlled by city government, it developed a plan to create jobs and increase tax revenues. The plan called for the purchase and demolition of the Fort Trumbull houses, after which private developers would build a resort hotel and conference center, research facilities, new homes, offices, and retail space where the Fort Trumbull houses had formerly stood.

New London began making deals to buy the properties in Fort Trumbull (there were 115 separate lots) for this purpose. When all was said and done, the owners of fifteen lots, including Kelo, refused to sell. New London then commenced eminent domain proceedings in order to force the holdouts to sell their properties. In response, Kelo and the other holdouts sued to protect their homes, claiming that the proceedings would violate their constitutional rights. Eventually, the Supreme Court agreed to hear the case.

Kelo's argument was this: the Fifth Amendment says the government can take private property for "public use," but this land was not being taken for that purpose — it was being taken to build what amounted to a privately owned commercial real estate development in the hope of increasing tax revenues and spurring economic growth. The Founding Fathers had drawn a line, and New London had stepped over it.

"Public Use" Becomes "Public Purpose"

In 2005, by a very contentious 5–4 margin, the Supreme Court ruled against Kelo and in favor of New London. The Supreme Court decided that the meaning of the phrase "public use" in the Constitution also included projects pursued for a "public purpose." Granted, the Court said, the New London project would not be used by the public, like a highway or water plant, but the Fort Trumbull lots were being taken to benefit the public as part of a carefully considered, comprehensive economic rejuvenation plan that would serve the public's need for new jobs and increased tax revenue. For five of the nine justices, that "public purpose" was enough of a "public use" to satisfy the Fifth Amendment.

Justice O'Connor wrote a vigorous dissenting opinion. "The specter of condemnation hangs over all property," she wrote. "Nothing is to prevent the state from replacing any Motel 6 with a Ritz-Carlton, any home with a shopping mall, or any farm with a factory." She was particularly troubled by the potential for what the decision would mean to citizens who did not wield power among public officials. "The beneficiaries are likely to be those citizens with disproportionate influence and power in the political process, including large corporations and development firms," O'Connor wrote. "As for the victims, the government now has license to transfer property from those with fewer resources to those with more. The founders cannot have intended this perverse result."

Justice Thomas stated his dissenting view with equal force: "Something has gone seriously awry with this Court's interpretation of the Constitution. Though citizens are safe from the government in their homes, the homes themselves are not."

The *Kelo* decision has been welcomed by state and local officials who have been struggling with economic redevelopment projects. At the same time, anti-*Kelo* forces are hard at work. Currently pending in the Senate is the Protection of Homes, Small Businesses, and Private Property Act of 2005 which, if passed, would prohibit use of the power of eminent domain for economic development projects. Similar bills have been introduced in the House and in various states. Whether those statutes are constitutional may be on the Supreme Court's docket in the near future.

In the meantime, there is good news and bad news. The good news is that it will be easier for federal, state, and local governments to pursue economic revitalization projects. The bad news is that, as part of the process, your backyard may end up in the middle of a factory or hotel lobby.

26. Monroe v. Pape

You Can Sue City Hall 1961

What happens when the government, which is responsible for creating the law, then violates the law? The Supreme Court sets limits on how far government can intrude into your life, but what are your rights if the government oversteps its boundaries?

As a practical matter, your right to hold the government accountable for its actions was uncertain and unpredictable, until the case of *Monroe v. Pape*. The *Monroe* case applies in a variety of contexts ranging from unlawful restrictions on businesses and property owners, to violations of the rights of criminal defendants. In any discussion concerning the boundaries of the government's power over businesses and individuals under the Due Process Clause, the Commerce Clause, or any other portion of the Constitution, *Monroe* answers the key question: what can those whose rights have been violated do about it?

In the *Monroe* case, thirteen Chicago police officers broke into the Monroe family's home in the early morning without a warrant, routed the occupants from bed, made them stand naked in the living room, and ransacked every room, emptying drawers and ripping mattress covers. Mr. Monroe was then taken to the police station, detained for ten hours while he was interrogated about a two-day-old murder without being permitted to call his family or attorney, and then released without criminal charges being brought against him.

Monroe sued the police officers for damages in federal court, under a post–Civil War statute generally referred to today as "Section 1983." Monroe chose this strategy, as opposed to filing a lawsuit in the local state court, because under state law his chances of successfully suing state officials or employees were slim, and he believed that local state court judges might be prone to protect local police officers. Section

1983, originally called "the Ku Klux Klan Act of 1871," was enacted by Congress to address the fact that many Southern states were refusing to protect freed blacks from whippings, lynchings, and other atrocities at the hands of whites, mainly Klan members. Monroe took the position that Section 1983 was more than an anachronism limited to the unusual circumstances of the post–Civil War era, and that it gave all persons whose constitutional rights were violated a federal right to sue for damages in federal court.

Using the Power of the Government
Against the Government

Monroe v. Pape eventually reached the Supreme Court, and, in a 1961 landmark ruling, Monroe won. The Supreme Court ruled that Section 1983 allowed individuals to bring federal court lawsuits for damages as the result of any "misuse of power" by state officials "clothed with the authority of state law." In 1971, the Supreme Court extended this ruling to allow claims in federal courts against not only state officials, but federal officials as well, in the case of *Bivens v. Six Unknown Named Agents of Federal Bureau of Narcotics.*

In the wake of *Monroe* and *Bivens*, literally thousands of Section 1983 cases have been successfully filed against government officials in federal courts for claimed violations of constitutional rights, such as actions based on unlawful searches, unlawful arrests, police brutality, arbitrary regulation of business and property, improper taxation, governmental dishonesty, and much more.

At their core, the *Monroe* and *Bivens* decisions allow individuals whose constitutional rights have been violated to use the power of the government against the government—a remarkable characteristic of our democracy that we have come to take for granted. This, in turn, has had a predictable effect on government accountability: faced with the prospect of having to explain their actions to a federal court jury, government officials become much more cautious before trifling with individual rights. For this reason, many commentators view *Monroe* and *Bivens* as being among the most significant decisions of the century.

CONSTITUTION
of the
UNITED STATES
of America.

Virtue Liberty and independence
Internal Improvements
U.S. Bank

CHAPTER 8

LIMITING THE IMPERIAL PRESIDENCY

"When the President does it, that means that it is not illegal."

—RICHARD M. NIXON

Those who have occupied the White House have frequently tried to expand the scope of their authority and power. Many have taken the position that the president is wholly independent and has the right to do what he thinks best, without having to answer to the other branches of government.

When the framers of the Constitution, steeped in English law, gathered in Philadelphia to debate and draft the Constitution, they were familiar with such governmental philosophies. For centuries, English law provided that "the king can do no wrong," and untold generations suffered the consequences of an unchecked monarchy. The English emasculated that principle when they enacted the Magna Carta in 1215, creating many of the fundamental rights that eventually found their way into our Constitution. To be sure, the framers had their disagreements over how powerful the president should be, but no one held out for the creation of an infallible monarchy—much, *very* much, the opposite.

The fact that the president *can* do wrong, however, raises difficult questions about our system of checks and balances. Who decides if the president is wrong? How do you keep politics out of the process? What if national security is at stake? Not surprisingly, it has been, and will continue to be, the Supreme Court that answers these questions.

A ca. 1833 caricature of President Andrew Jackson as a despotic monarch, probably issued during the fall of 1833 in response to the president's September order to remove federal deposits from the Bank of the United States.

27. Youngstown Sheet & Tube Co. v. Sawyer

The Steel-Seizure Case: How Far Can the President Go in the Name of National Security? 1952

In June 1950, North Korea invaded South Korea, and the Korean War was on. As the conflict raged, the collective bargaining agreement between the United Steel Workers and the steel industry was due to expire, and the union demanded a substantial raise, which the steel industry refused. Attempts at settlement failed, and on April 4, 1952, the union gave notice of a nationwide steel strike to commence on April 9, 1952.

Steel was an indispensable component of the war effort, and President Truman believed that a work stoppage would jeopardize national security. Citing his authority under "the Constitution and laws of the United States, and as President of the United States and Commander in Chief of the Armed Forces," just a few hours before the strike was to begin Truman issued an executive order directing Secretary of Commerce Charles Sawyer to seize the steel mills from their owners. Truman explained his actions to the American people in a radio and television address, speaking of the grave dangers that would face the nation if the steel companies ceased production.

Less than an hour after Truman concluded his broadcast, attorneys for the steel companies appeared at the home of a federal trial court judge in Washington, D.C., and requested an injunction prohibiting Truman's actions. They rightly pointed out that Congress had never passed a law authorizing a president to unilaterally seize control of an industry, no matter the circumstances, and they asked that their property be returned to them immediately. What, they asked, were the limits of the president's power?

The conflict gave rise to the case of *Youngstown Sheet & Tube Co. v. Sawyer*, better known as the Steel Seizure Case. In the midst of blaring headlines and a rancorous national debate, it was once again left to the judiciary to write the rule book by which Congress and the president would be authorized to govern the country. The issues in the Steel Seizure Case were of such importance that the Supreme Court heard and decided the case just two months after the steel companies' lawyers appeared at the trial court judge's Washington home.

When the case got to the Supreme Court, Truman, through government lawyers, argued for the supremacy of the executive branch: in times of national emergency, the president has the power, and even the obligation, to step in and take action, and neither the Congress nor the judiciary has the constitutional right to stop him. Truman's argument did not depend on legal niceties. When there is a true crisis, he contended, a president must have the right to do what he thinks is right, without having to seek and wait for approval from the other branches of government.

The Supreme Court disagreed. After hearing two days of oral argument, it ruled against Truman by a 6–3 vote.

The "Zone of Twilight"

Justice Black wrote the majority opinion. He began with the foundational proposition that a president is not all-powerful, no matter the circumstances. A president cannot take action, said Justice Black, unless that action is authorized either by a statute passed by Congress, or the Constitution. Plainly, there was no statute authorizing a president to unilaterally seize private property (let alone an entire industry); whatever statutory authority there was *protected* private property from governmental seizure. The question, then, was whether the Constitution itself empowered Truman to seize the steel mills.

Truman's lawyers focused on Article II of the Constitution, which appoints the president as the commander in chief. They contended that the commander in chief must have broad, expansive powers, as would a general on a battlefield. Justice Black, in terse language, rejected this argument, and ruled that the power of a commander in chief cannot extend so far as to allow the taking of private property in the name of national security. "This," he said, "is a job for the Nation's lawmakers, not its military authorities."

Justice Jackson, while concurring in the overall result, wrote a separate opinion which, over the years, has become much more influential than Justice Black's reasoning. Justice Jackson wrote that a president's powers are at their maximum when he seeks to enforce plainly expressed congressional will, and those powers are at their "lowest ebb" when he seeks to act against the will of Congress. But, he said, "there is a zone of twilight" between these extremes, and the limits of presidential power in these gray areas "is likely to depend on the imperatives of events"—that is, the president has some room to move in cases of true national emergency, so long as he does not directly violate the plainly expressed will of the Congress.

Justice Jackson concluded that Congress had in prior laws forbidden unilateral seizures of property, and for that reason Truman's actions had to be overturned. But the implication was that if Congress had not plainly expressed its will on this very issue—that is, if Truman had been operating in the "zone of twilight"—Truman might well have been free to do as he thought best in view of the national security issues he faced. The message to both future members of Congress and future presidents was unmistakable.

Truman immediately complied with the Supreme Court's ruling. A fifty-three-day steel strike ensued, no steel shortage occurred, and a settlement was ultimately reached.

National Security Versus Civil Rights:
The Beat Goes On

How far a president can go in the name of national security, and the extent to which Congress can rein in executive powers during such times, has always been and will remain a vital national issue of daunting complexity. There is, of course, no singular formula that can define the proper spheres of executive and congressional authority in all circumstances — particularly when, as is so often the case, the dispute resides in the "zone of twilight" described by Justice Jackson.

As recently as 2004, however, the Supreme Court again stressed that the president's powers are limited by law, even in wartime. Justice O'Connor, referencing the Steel Seizure Case, made quick work of President Bush's contention that he could hold suspected terrorists without a hearing. "We have long since made clear that a state of war is not a blank check for the president when it comes to the rights of the Nation's citizens."

In 2005 and 2006, the Steel Seizure Case again took center stage during the confirmation hearings for Justice Alito and the Senate hearings on the Bush administration's domestic surveillance programs. Senator Arlen Specter stated at the commencement of the Alito hearing: "This hearing comes at a time of great national concern about the balance between civil rights and the president's national security authority." He went on to say, "The president's constitutional war powers as commander in chief to conduct electronic surveillance appear to conflict with congressional legislation in the Foreign Intelligence Surveillance

Act. This conflict could activate the considerations raised in Justice Jackson's historic concurrence in the Youngstown Steel Seizure Case. . . . It is a critical analysis for, as Justice Jackson noted: 'What is at stake is the equilibrium established by our constitutional system.'"

The Steel Seizure Case continues to give Congress and the judiciary ample ammunition with which to challenge an exercise of presidential power that arguably oversteps legal boundaries. How such confrontations are resolved in the future will depend on an array of variables, such as whether the challenged presidential action impinges on individual civil liberties, whether it affects only foreign affairs or also domestic affairs, the immediacy and risks of the crisis at hand, and, of course, the personal predilections, backgrounds, and philosophies of the justices who make up the Supreme Court at any given time.

28. United States v. Nixon

Nixon, *Executive Privilege, and the* Watergate Scandal *1974*

Can the president withhold information from Congress merely because he is the president? Can the president override congressional efforts to oversee the legality of what he does? The inglorious Watergate scandal ultimately forced the Supreme Court to confront these issues in the most dramatic constitutional crisis since the Civil War.

A "Third-Rate Burglary"

In June 1972, during the Nixon-McGovern presidential campaign, five men with cameras and listening devices were arrested inside the Democratic National Committee's offices, located in the Watergate complex in Washington. Thanks in large part to dogged investigative reporting by the *Washington Post* (as portrayed in the book and movie *All the President's Men*), the burglars were publicly linked to Nixon's reelection committee and administration officials. Despite the administration's denials of any involvement (Nixon's press secretary dismissed the break-in as "a third-rate burglary"), public pressure mounted, and a Senate committee conducted an investigation, followed by hearings in 1973.

The hearings were televised, and they captivated the nation. As millions of citizens watched, various Nixon administration officials, including John Dean, Nixon's former counsel, claimed that Nixon's closest associates—and perhaps Nixon himself—had orchestrated a cover-up of the break-in and engaged in a host of other illegal activities. Nixon was clearly in the Senate's sights: Senator Howard Baker repeatedly asked witnesses the question that has since worked its way into the nation's political lexicon: "What did the president know, and when did he know it?"

During an otherwise routine July 1973 hearing session, one of Nixon's assistants, Alexander Butterfield, revealed that Nixon had installed a taping system in the Oval Office and had retained possession of the very tapes that would definitively and undeniably answer Senator Baker's famous question. Butterfield's revelation changed the nature of the Senate inquiry—why ask witnesses what Nixon had been told and what he had said in the Oval Office, when there existed the ultimate original source material, a tape recording?

The "Saturday Night Massacre"

By this time, honoring a promise he had made during his Senate confirmation hearings, Attorney General Elliot Richardson had appointed Archibald Cox, a well-known lawyer, to serve as a special prosecutor investigating the Watergate case. Shortly after Butterfield's testimony, Cox served a subpoena on the White House, demanding the tapes. The battle was under way.

Nixon refused to produce the tapes, citing a murky legal doctrine known as "executive privilege." He contended that each branch of government was separate from the other and legally entitled to be free from interference by the other. In fact, Nixon knew that, among many other embarrassments, the tapes included the "smoking gun," conversations in which Nixon sought to use the CIA to unlawfully obstruct the FBI's investigation of the Watergate burglary in the effort to hide the involvement of his administration and, perhaps, himself.

Nixon offered Cox a compromise involving a screening of the tapes by a Nixon senatorial ally and the production of edited versions. Cox refused.

The next night, October 23, 1973, a Saturday, Nixon ordered Attorney General Richardson to fire Cox. In view of the promise he had made to Congress, Richardson refused and, in protest, resigned. Nixon then ordered Deputy Attorney General William Ruckelshaus to fire Cox. Ruckelshaus refused, and resigned as well. Nixon then ordered the Solicitor General, Robert Bork, to fire Cox. Bork was, by default, now in charge of the Justice Department and he, too, considered resigning. Bork, unlike Richardson, would not be violating a commitment to the Senate if he obeyed the order, and Richardson persuaded him to comply, for fear that the Justice Department would otherwise be thrown into turmoil. Bork reluctantly fired Cox, culminating what has been dubbed the "Saturday Night Massacre."

Congress was outraged, and various bills of impeachment were eventually introduced, charging the president with, among other things, abuses of power and obstruction of justice. The battle had escalated into a full-fledged war between Congress and the president.

The firing of Cox did Nixon no good and a lot of harm. Cox's successor, Leon Jaworski, doggedly pushed for the production of the tapes, and public pressure crescendoed. Nixon backpedaled, releasing edited transcripts of the tapes. The transcripts corroborated much of what Dean and many witnesses had stated, and also included a very suspicious eighteen-minute gap, which Nixon blamed on his secretary, further fanning public cynicism and outrage.

Jaworski sought a court order compelling Nixon to obey the subpoena. Now all three branches of government were involved in the conflagration. Nixon again relied on "executive privilege," arguing that neither he nor any other president could fulfill the duties of the office if private conversations and planning sessions were subject to public disclosure. Nixon contended that he led a separate branch of government, and that the other branches, Congress and the courts, had no right to compel him to take actions he felt to be unwarranted.

The lower courts entered orders, appeals were filed, and a major constitutional crisis loomed. It ultimately fell to the Supreme Court to define the boundaries of congressional, presidential, and judicial power.

The Supreme Court's Decision:
A President, Not a Monarch

It is now known that as they debated the case, the justices had substantial disagreements among themselves, but agreed that they had to speak with one voice. Nixon had publicly agreed to accept a "definitive" order from the Court, and the justices feared that if their opinion were not unanimous, Nixon would use that as a basis on which to defy the Court's order. This raised the specter of Congress and the Court sending federal marshals to remove the tapes from the White House, and the president, as commander in chief, mustering armed forces to guard the Oval Office. It was a risk the Court knew it could not take, and the justices managed to set aside their differences and reach a unanimous and clear result.

Chief Justice Warren Burger announced the Court's decision on July 24, 1974: Nixon was ordered to surrender the tapes.

The Court recognized that a president could insist on a right to confidentiality in some circumstances, such as to protect national security—a concept later presidents have attempted to use when called upon to disclose their personal documents and records. Nixon, however, had not sought to avoid the subpoena on these grounds but, rather, claimed that executive privilege was absolute, that as the leader of an independent branch of government he could withhold what he wanted. Nixon's lawyer explained Nixon's position in his argument before the Supreme Court: "The President wants me to argue that he is as powerful a monarch as Louis XIV, only four years at a time, and is not subject to the processes of any court in the land except the court of impeachment."

The Supreme Court disagreed, ruling that a president is not above the law, and, when faced with a subpoena issued to obtain evidence in an investigation of national importance with criminal implications, he must comply, as must any other citizen.

To his credit, Nixon complied less than a week later. The House Judiciary Committee had already begun impeachment proceedings, and Nixon knew that the evidence on the tapes would seal his fate. On August 8, 1974, reading the writing on the wall, Nixon resigned—the first president ever to do so. Vice President Gerald Ford assumed the presidency.

After being sworn in by Chief Justice Burger, President Ford announced that "our long national nightmare is over." As much as anything else, the "nightmare" was the prospect that the branches of government would defy each other, and that their disagreements could, literally, result in a confrontation of force. That did not happen, leading President Ford to emotionally, and correctly, observe, "Our Constitution works; our great Republic is a government of laws and not of men."

On September 8, 1974, Ford pardoned Nixon for any crimes he might have committed in the Watergate affair.

29. Boumediene v. Bush and Al Odah v. U.S.

Who Writes the Rules of War? 2008

In retrospect, it seems right that President Truman should not have had the unilateral authority to nationalize an entire industry by edict, and that President Nixon should not have had the right to cloak the presidency with the prerogatives of eighteenth-century monarchs. Our traditions respect strong leadership but disdain power grabs. In situations like these, there is something in our American DNA that calls out for the Supreme Court to intervene and recalibrate the delicate balance between the powers of presidents and the rule of law.

But what about the conduct of wars? The Constitution establishes the president as the commander in chief and provides Congress with wartime funding and oversight responsibilities. Does the Supreme Court have the right to look over their shoulders and review how the president and Congress choose to fight?

A New Kind of War

Shortly after the 9/11 attacks, the Bush administration began a global effort to round up suspected terrorists. It cast a wide net—such is the difficulty of fighting dispersed armies of nonuniformed twenty-first-century terrorists—and many people who had done little more than occupy the wrong place at the wrong time were ensnared.

According to international law, "enemy combatants" can be held as prisoners of war. But under the Geneva Convention, those who claim not to be enemy combatants are to be given a full hearing, including basic rights of due process, so they have an opportunity to prove their innocence.

Many of the suspects rounded up after 9/11 claimed that they were not enemy combatants, and yet, they were imprisoned without any hearing. The Bush administration offered an explanation based on practicalities. Unlike conventional warfare, where uniformed enemy combatants can be captured on the battlefield, terrorists fade into the background, often far from the scenes of their crimes, and it can be impossible to tell the terrorists from the bystanders. The full-scale hearings contemplated by the Geneva Convention could no longer be justified, and would compromise fundamental antiterrorism strategies. Thousands of lives were at risk: the terrorists were fighting a new kind of war; the old rules of law no longer applied.

The Bush administration suspected that it might be on thin legal ice, and its lawyers struggled to find a way to further justify its position. They did not have much to go on; but, ultimately, they crafted (some would say manufactured) a legal rationale. Initially, they contended that the Geneva Convention only applies to combatants who fight for nations that have signed it, and not to terrorists who are affiliated with no government and can surface from virtually anywhere. But recognizing that U.S. courts might not agree, they also argued that noncitizen foreign detainees do not have the right to challenge their status and treatment in our judicial system—and even if they did, they most certainly had no such right if they were held overseas, not on American soil. In effect, the position espoused by the Bush administration lawyers was, "we might be wrong, but there's nothing the detainees can do about it."

Based on these legal positions, the Bush administration constructed a terrorist detention facility at the U.S. naval base at Guantanamo Bay, Cuba; continued to hold the detainees without hearings; and steadfastly claimed that whatever went on there was outside the reach of American law . . . whatever happens in Guantanamo, stays in Guantanamo. One administration official told the press that Guantanamo was the legal equivalent of "outer space."

The Governmental Face-off Begins

The expected legal challenges were filed shortly after the first detainees arrived at Guantanamo in early 2002. By 2004, the first wave of these cases had made their way to the Supreme Court which, in the case of *Rasul v. Bush*, dealt the Bush administration a stinging setback: the Court ruled that American officials could not lock up foreign detainees, whether in the United States or in Guantanamo, without some demonstrated reason, and that the foreign detainees had a right to a reasonable military commission hearing so they could challenge the accusations being made against them. U.S. officials acting in the name of the U.S. government must comply with U.S. law, no matter where they conduct their business.

The Bush administration (along with much of Congress) acted immediately to parry the Supreme Court's thrust. It initiated military-run "combatant status review tribunals" (CSRTs), to ostensibly provide the detainees with a military commission hearing that satisfied legal standards. In fact, however, the CSRTs ran hearings in name only—they were one-sided proceedings, held in secrecy, in which the detainees were given virtually no rights to review and confront whatever evidence the military chose to present against them.

In 2006, the Supreme Court agreed to review a challenge to the CSRTs in the case of *Hamdan v. Rumsfeld.* Hamdan was a Yemeni national who admitted that he had at one time been Osama bin Laden's driver, but who denied any terrorist activities.

In *Hamdan*, a bare majority of the Supreme Court saw the situation as another *Youngstown Sheet & Tube* case. The Uniform Code of

Military Justice, enacted by Congress long before, required military commissions such as the CSRTs to comply with the Geneva Convention, which mandated hearings that included a meaningful right to challenge and present evidence. Faced with what it saw as a plain expression of congressional will, the majority reined in President Bush just as it had reined in President Truman: the executive branch is not free to disregard Congress except in the face of truly exigent circumstances, the Court said, and there was no proof that national security would be compromised if Guantanamo detainees were afforded a fair hearing at which they had a genuine opportunity to prove that they were not terrorists.

The dissenters disagreed, calling the majority's view "patently erroneous." They argued that such matters were outside the Supreme Court's sphere of influence, and stressed that the *Youngstown Sheet & Tube* decision, properly interpreted, required "a heavy measure of deference" to the president, the commander in chief, in time of real war. This was serious business in which judges have no place, they stressed, and the Supreme Court needed to stay out of it.

The ball was back in the Bush administration's court, and at the president's urging Congress quickly passed another law, the Military Commissions Act. It added a bit more due process to the proceedings, but essentially left the Bush administration's system intact. Now the legal fundamentals had shifted: no longer could the president be charged with disregarding the will of Congress; instead, the president and the Congress were on precisely the same page.

In response, a new lawsuit was filed, involving thirty-seven Guantanamo detainees. The case was brought in the name of two of them: Lakhdar Boumediene, an Algerian taken from Bosnia in October 2001; and Fawzi Khalid Abdullah Fahad Al Odah, a Kuwaiti captured in Afghanistan in 2001. Both claimed they were innocent, and they each sought a hearing so they could prove it.

The *Boumediene* and *Al Odah* cases crystallized a different issue, involving the fundamentals of our tripartite form of government. In *Hamdan*, the Supreme Court had served as a sort of governmental referee—it found that the executive branch had gone rogue and improperly overstepped the directives of the legislative branch. But now the executive and legislative branches had joined forces. In times of war, shouldn't that be good enough? Does the Supreme Court have the right to tell the other branches how to fight a war?

The rule of law applies in both war and peace, said the lawyers representing the detainees. The fact that the president and the Congress now agree does not end the inquiry. The *real* question is this: does their agreement violate the Constitution? The Supreme Court has both the power and the obligation to answer that question, they argued. It cannot sit on the sidelines.

Still, as the dissenters had argued in *Hamdan*, was this, the conduct of war, really any of the Supreme Court's business? Doesn't there come a point when national security trumps constitutional niceties?

The "Great Writ"

The *Boumediene* and *Al Odah* cases focused squarely on the bedrock constitutional right of "habeas corpus." Habeas corpus (Latin for "you have the body") has deep roots in fundamental Anglo-American traditions. Rightly known as the "Great Writ," it was originally conceived as a means to keep the Crown from arbitrarily imprisoning its enemies without due process. Today, it remains a bodyguard of key personal freedoms—anyone being held in custody can file a habeas corpus petition and have an independent judge review the legality of his detention. If, for instance, a police officer or district attorney locks you up because of a personal vendetta, or because of your race or religion, or to quell political opposition, or based on phony evidence, habeas corpus is your last (and often best) line of defense. It is designed to be the constitutional antidote to injustices involving personal liberty, and the Constitution itself mandates that it may be suspended only in the case of "rebellion or invasion."

If the right of habeas corpus provides anything, the *Boumediene* and *Al Odah* lawyers argued, it provides people like the detainees in Guantanamo with the right to challenge the government's decision to imprison them without a proven reason to do so. Yes, we're involved in a war on terrorism, but fundamental rights remain fundamental rights, no matter the unpopularity of those who seek to assert them. Indeed, the right of habeas corpus was designed to protect the very people the government would prefer to leave unprotected.

But, still, an overriding issue remained: do foreigners—noncitizens who have never set foot on American soil, who were captured as part of the government's efforts to prevent another terrorist attack, and who are being held offshore by the military during wartime—have the right of habeas corpus?

On the one hand, the president and Congress have the constitutional responsibility to defend the nation, and the military has the acknowledged expertise. Can habeas corpus be used to subject their decisions to review by judges who sit safely behind a mahogany bench?

But on the other hand, there *is* the Constitution. Are the risks to national security even greater if we allow the very persons and institutions sworn to defend the Constitution to erode the rights it provides?

The Ruling: A Constitution without Boundaries

In a 5–4 decision replete with strident, sometimes apocalyptic dissents, the Supreme Court ruled that the Constitution's reach was limited by neither geography nor war, and it does not allow the government to imprison *anyone*, citizen or noncitizen, in war or peace, domestically or abroad, without the basic due process civilized societies recognize as being elemental to any meaningful effort to find the truth. The Court ruled that the one-sided hearings implemented by the Bush administration were fundamentally unfair and, in the absence of lawful military commission hearings, the Guantanamo detainees (and, by plain implication, detainees being held as suspected terrorists anywhere else in the world) *did* have a habeas corpus right under the Constitution to challenge their detention in United States civilian courts.

Justice Anthony Kennedy, writing for the majority, summarized his view of the inevitable conflicts between national security and individual liberties that brought the Guantanamo detainees before the nation's highest court: "The laws and Constitution are designed to survive, and remain in force, in extraordinary times." The branches of government, he warned, may not "switch the Constitution on or off at will."

Chief Justice Roberts attacked the majority for not allowing the bipartisan legislation crafted by the executive and legislative branches to be fully implemented and vetted by lower courts before being dismantled by the Supreme Court. He charged that the majority was more concerned about flexing its judicial muscles than protecting the detainees. The ruling, he concluded, "is not really about the detainees at all, but about control of federal policy regarding enemy combatants." He expressed concern that the public will "lose a bit more control over the conduct of this nation's foreign policy to unelected, politically unaccountable judges."

Justice Scalia was less diplomatic. He excoriated the majority's ruling—the unique nature of terrorism requires military, not judicial solutions, he reasoned—and he predicted that "devastating" and "disastrous consequences" would flow from the decision. "It will almost certainly cause more Americans to be killed."

Justice Kennedy was not moved. Obviously influenced by the fact that many of the detainees had been imprisoned for six years without any meaningful hearing, he concluded that the Supreme Court had to act without further delay. "Within the Constitution's separation-of-powers structure, few exercises of judicial power are as legitimate or as necessary as the responsibility to hear challenges to the authority of the Executive to imprison a person."

Will Terrorists Go Free?

Contrary to some reports, the decision does *not* mean that the Guantanamo detainees must be released; it means only that they (and other detainees, no matter where held) are entitled to a hearing, including the basic rights and safeguards Americans take for granted, for the purpose of determining whether they are enemy combatants or innocent bystanders. The alternative is the endorsement of a policy in which suspected combatants are held indefinitely, like prisoners in a dungeon, until we unilaterally determine what to do with them.

But what about the practicalities and the real, palpable national security concerns? The government will bear the burden of proving that there is a basis to continue to hold each of the detainees, if it cannot do so, then they *will* be freed. Will our government be forced to disclose classified information and intelligence-gathering techniques in order to prove its case? Proving that a farmer is also a terrorist can be difficult: where will the evidence come from? Will our most covert and specialized military and intelligence personnel be forced to testify and undergo cross-examination about what they know and how they know it? What if a terrorist confessed to an American interrogator, but without having been given a Miranda warning? Suppose a detainee, while not a terrorist himself, has crucial information: will that be a basis on which continued detention is permitted? Will information obtained through so-called "coercive" interrogation methods be admissible? If there's solid evidence that an individual is a terrorist, but we can't fully prove it, will the individual be set free, no matter the security risks?

This is where rhetoric and practicalities collide. It will not be easy.

So What? How Does This Affect *Your* Life?

Why would two cases dealing with the rights of suspected terrorists being held in Cuba be included in a book that focuses on the Supreme Court cases that most directly affect *your* life?

Consider this question on two levels.

First, in the coming years, few things may affect the lives of Americans more than the success or failure of our efforts to defeat international terrorism. A keystone of those efforts has been measures designed to win the so-called "hearts and minds" of the populations in which terrorism flourishes by convincing them that democracies in general, and America in particular, respect individual freedoms and promote justice. The message is that there is a better way, our way. But many analysts believe that institutions like Guantanamo have inexorably eroded our credibility by displaying to the world that in reality we do not practice what we preach: rather than standing for fundamental liberties and human rights, Guantanamo has allowed our adversaries to convincingly portray us as a society that incarcerates individuals on the basis of mere suspicion without a meaningful effort to determine if that incarceration is warranted.

Will the fact that we will now afford the detainees full and honest due process hearings, and that we will close Guantanamo, change that perception and elevate our standing among those we seek to influence?

Will whatever salutary effects the decision produces be counterbalanced by the release of dangerous terrorists, or by the extent to which it may hamstring the military's effort to obtain crucial intelligence and take terrorists out of circulation? There is, of course, no way to know, and much will depend on the related policies adopted by future administrations.

But both the Supreme Court majority and the minority agree on this: the decision represents a searing rebuke of the way both the executive and the Congress have conducted themselves since 9/11, and it will have a major effect on how the government conducts itself in the future, for better (if you believe the majority) or worse (if you believe the minority).

Second, whether justified (as the majority contends) or unjustified (as the minority contends), the decision represents an *extremely* significant assertion of Supreme Court authority in respect to the president and the Congress—some commentators, perhaps a bit overwrought, have called it the most significant redefinition of the balance of power in at least a half century. Will the Supreme Court's refusal to yield to presidential or congressional judgments on national security continue? Will rulings on the constitutionality of "coercive interrogation techniques" and other tactics used in the war on terror be next? Will an emboldened Supreme Court expand its reach into other areas of international policy? Or is the *Boumediene* and *Al Odah* decision an aberration that is limited to the unusual and extreme plight of some of the Guantanamo detainees?

Many of these questions are approached in the final chapter, where the future of the Supreme Court is discussed. A one-justice switch could turn the 5–4 majority that decided the case into a minority, dissenting view, potentially turning the principles underlying the *Boumediene* and *Al Odah* decision on their heads—and further documenting that there is a vast array of reasons why American citizens should be vitally concerned about who the next Supreme Court justice may be.

CHAPTER 9

HOW FREE IS FREE SPEECH?

*"If liberty means anything at all, it means the right
to tell people what they do not want to hear."*

—GEORGE ORWELL,
BRITISH AUTHOR AND JOURNALIST

The First Amendment prohibits the government from "abridging the freedom of speech." It is difficult to overstate the importance of this precept to the Founding Fathers and to our survival as a democracy.

But as the aphorism about yelling "Fire!" in a crowded theater makes evident, free speech cannot always be so free. Speech, for instance, can take the form of calls to violence and anarchy, endangering entire communities. Speech can be obscene past the point of imagining and repugnant to the values that holds a society intact. Speech can endanger children.

Underregulation of speech can be dangerous. Overregulation of speech can be more dangerous. It is the Supreme Court's unenviable job to determine where you draw the line.

A group of diverse Americans raises the Old Glory in this poster commemorating the Fourth of July, 1876; is burning this flag an act of free speech?

30. Brandenburg v. Ohio

The Right to Be Repugnant 1969

In the 1960s, Clarence Brandenburg was a well-known leader of an Ohio Ku Klux Klan group. He invited a reporter to film various Klan activities, such as a cross-burning attended by armed men. In the film, Brandenburg, in Klan regalia, made a speech threatening vengeance if the president, Congress, and Supreme Court "continues to suppress the white, Caucasian race." Brandenburg also advocated that blacks be transported to Africa and Jews be sent to Israel.

In the early 1900s, Ohio, like nineteen other states, enacted what was then known as a "criminal syndicalism" statute. Ohio's statute made it a crime to advocate "the duty, necessity, or propriety of crime, sabotage, violence, or unlawful methods of terrorism as a means of accomplishing industrial or political reform," and to assemble with a group for such purposes. After the film became public, Brandenburg was arrested and convicted under the Ohio statute, and sentenced to a fine and imprisonment.

Brandenburg challenged the constitutionality of the Ohio statute, claiming that it infringed on his basic First Amendment right to free speech. The Ohio courts turned down Brandenburg's appeal, and the Supreme Court then agreed to hear the case.

Only in America: The Right to Advocate Revolution

In its 1969 decision in *Brandenburg v. Ohio*, the Supreme Court unanimously invalidated Brandenburg's conviction. The Court ruled that "mere advocacy" is free speech protected by the First Amendment and it cannot be punished—even when the speaker is advocating the use of force or the violation of law. Only advocacy that is "directed to inciting or producing imminent lawless action and is likely to incite or produce such action" can be restricted—what courts often call "fighting words." This is a crucial, constitutional line in the sand, and the Court ruled that any law or act of a government official that fails to appreciate this distinction "sweeps within its condemnation speech which our Constitution has immunized from governmental control."

Brandenburg exemplifies how far the Supreme Court will go to insulate speech from government interference, a perspective that carries over into many other arenas, such as the Court's reluctance to delve as deeply into the regulation of obscenity as many people feel it should. The decision stands as the Supreme Court's last word on the broad protections the First Amendment provides to speech that advocates force or lawlessness to effectuate social change.

Fundamentally, *Brandenburg* provides a constitutional safe haven for virtually all speech that communicates an idea or position, no matter how repugnant. Our traditions so respect the right of free speech that our government will protect even those who espouse that it be overthrown.

31. Miller v. California

Obscenity and the First Amendment 1973

One of the linchpins of a democratic society is this: people must know, clearly and in advance, what conduct can be prosecuted by the government as a crime, and what conduct is lawful. If the definitions are vague and blurry, the government can arrest whomever they don't like whenever they wish, and citizens must walk on eggshells for fear of recrimination, which is how dictatorships remain in power. Few scenarios could be more violative of the "government of laws, not men" envisioned by the Constitution.

"I Know It When I See It"

Decades ago, the Supreme Court ruled that "obscenity" is not protected by the First Amendment. What that meant as a practical matter was that the federal and state governments could make it a crime to distribute obscene materials, which is exactly what was happening. But how can "obscenity" be defined so that people might know, clearly and in advance, what they could do without risking a jail term? Without a clear definition, the local bookseller would risk a criminal record if he failed to remove from the shelves all of the novels with graphic love scenes (*Madame Bovary? Lolita? Ulysses?*), and the local theater would have to think twice before showing a movie with sexual content (*The Graduate?*). And what about the rights of adults to do what they want in their private lives without the government's "Big Brother" interference?

In a 1964 case, Justice Potter Stewart was asked to decide whether a movie under the Court's review was "hard core pornography," and he mirrored the maddening difficulty of trying to define what may be indefinable. "I shall not today attempt further to define the kinds of material I understand to be embraced within that shorthand description; and perhaps I could never succeed in intelligibly doing so," he said. "But I know it when I see it, and the motion picture involved in this case is not that."

The "I know it when I see it" test was not exactly the kind of standard that would provide fair notice of the activities that might land you in jail. But Justice Stewart's frustration was understandable: how can words draw clear lines between what is and is not obscene, any more than words can define what is and is not beautiful, or does or does not taste good?

"Movie Day" in the Supreme Court

The upshot of a rule that says you can only know obscenity when you see obscenity is that, eventually, you have to look at obscenity—and through the 1960s that's just what the Supreme Court justices did.

According to various articles and books about the Supreme Court (often based on accounts from former Supreme Court law clerks), many of the justices and their clerks regularly gathered in the Supreme Court basement on what came to be known as "movie days" to review films that were the subject of obscenity prosecutions. Some justices refused to participate. Others took it as a solemn duty. But a few seemed to enjoy their work. Justice Thurgood Marshall, it was said, sat in the front row and joked loudly, even asking for copies of films so he could show his children when they were older. Justice John Marshall Harlan II, who was nearly blind, mischievously sat next to more prudish colleagues and insisted that they narrate the on-screen goings-on, to his great amusement ("Oh, extraordinary!" he would frequently exclaim).

By the early 1970s, the Supreme Court was ready to find a different solution.

Let Someone Else Do It

In 1973, the Supreme Court again tackled the obscenity issue in the case of *Miller v. California*, which continues to represent the last, definitive word on the subject—at least to the extent a 5–4 decision can be "definitive."

Miller was convicted under a California obscenity statute for knowingly selling brochures that displayed men and women engaged in sexual activity. The law at the time stemmed from a 1957 case, *Roth v. United States*. Under *Roth*, in order to be obscene, a court had to find that the "dominant theme taken as a whole appeals to the prurient interest" of the "average person, applying contemporary community standards." Later cases added that only materials that are "patently offensive" and "utterly without redeeming social value" could be obscene.

By 1970, two of the sitting justices, Douglas and Black, believed the First Amendment protected *all* speech, including obscenity, and Justice William Brennan, who had written the *Roth* opinion, had concluded that efforts at definition were fruitless and counterproductive. Chief Justice Burger, however, believed that a framework should be developed that permitted localities to create their own obscenity standards, and he politicked among the justices for a majority vote in favor of that position.

What emerged from an extremely contentious debate among the justices was a bare majority in favor of a three-part test that would define what could be prosecuted as "obscenity":

(a) whether the average person, applying contemporary community standards, would find that the work, taken as a whole, appeals to the prurient interest,

(b) whether the work depicts or describes, in a patently offensive way, sexual conduct specifically defined by the applicable
state law, and

(c) whether the work, taken as a whole, lacks serious literary,
artistic, political, or scientific value.

If all three criteria were met, the work could be considered obscene,
and those who distributed it could be charged with a crime.

In effect, the Supreme Court, while setting some definitional limits,
abdicated responsibility for defining obscenity. The upshot of *Miller*
was to permit each locality to impose its own definition. What a jury in
one locality might consider "prurient" might be considered "literature"
in another.

Justice Stewart would no longer be able to know it when he saw it; it
would depend on where he was at the time.

Making Obscenity a Federal Case:
The New Wave of Prosecutions

The *Miller* decision resulted in literally hundreds of obscenity prosecutions in the few years after the case was decided, until the dust settled
and the rules of the game in each community became better known.
For many years thereafter, obscenity cases were rare.

That all changed in 2001, when the Bush administration began
bringing federal obscenity prosecutions. By way of comparison, there
were four obscenity prosecutions during the eight years of the Clinton
administration. Between 2001 and mid-2005, the Bush administration
obtained more than forty obscenity convictions. Given *Miller*'s focus on
community standards, the prosecutions were most often brought in

communities believed to be more traditionally conservative, making the prospect of obtaining a conviction more likely. In December 2005, for instance, a Florida man was sentenced to five years in prison by a federal judge in Montana for distributing obscene videotapes throughout the country.

Where all this leaves the obscenity issue may become extremely interesting in the near future. Given the important First Amendment questions that obscenity questions raise, one or more of the Bush administration's obscenity prosecutions could easily find their way to the Supreme Court.

Senators, congressmen, and the media consistently speak of the "conservative" tilt of the Supreme Court in recent years, particularly in view of recent appointments. But the "conservative" label has a different meaning when applied to a Supreme Court justice than it does when used in a political context. A "conservative" politician is often understood as one who favors more "traditional" values, and would seek to prohibit the distribution of sexually explicit materials. A "conservative" jurist, however, is typically regarded as one who takes laws in general, and the Constitution in particular, more literally, without attempting to inject personal values or notions of social justice.

The First Amendment says that the government "shall make no law . . . abridging the freedom of speech." It does not say that the government may make some laws. No law. We may soon see just how "conservative" the Supreme Court really is.

32. Texas v. Johnson

The Flag Burning Case: Can Conduct Be "Free Speech"? 1989

The First Amendment protects "freedom of speech," but people often communicate and express themselves in nonverbal ways. For that reason, the Supreme Court has, for many years, recognized that conduct, like gestures or demonstrations, can have a communicative element, and can be "speech" for First Amendment purposes. For instance, the Supreme Court has ruled that when, in the context of a political protest, a student wears a black armband to school in violation of school rules, the student is plainly attempting to communicate an idea, and the armband is "speech" entitled to First Amendment protection.

But how about burning the American flag? Just how far does the First Amendment go?

During the 1984 Republican National Convention in Dallas, Gregory Lee Johnson participated in a demonstration against the Reagan administration and its policies. The demonstration culminated at Dallas City Hall, where Johnson unfurled an American flag, doused it with kerosene, and set it on fire while others chanted "America, the red, white and blue, we spit on you." No one was injured or threatened, but many were seriously offended.

Johnson was arrested and convicted under a Texas statute, similar to statutes in forty-seven other states, prohibiting the desecration of the flag. He appealed his conviction, and the Supreme Court agreed to hear his case in 1989.

Johnson contended that the Texas statute violated his First Amendment rights of free speech. Johnson argued that what he did was not just an act of meaningless destruction, but was clearly meant to convey a political message protected by the First Amendment.

Texas argued that flag burning cannot be construed as "speech," but even if it were, not all "speech" is protected. The Supreme Court had long ago ruled that speech intended to incite imminent violence or other public harm does not merit First Amendment protection. Texas argued that flag desecration fell within this exception to the First Amendment: the flag represented the nation itself and, consequently, the desecration of the flag was so offensive to so many people that it always involved the threat of violence.

Can Setting a Fire Be "Speech"?

By a bare 5–4 majority, the Supreme Court agreed with Johnson and ruled the Texas statute unconstitutional. Justice Brennan wrote, "If there is a bedrock principle underlying the First Amendment, it is that the Government may not prohibit the expression of an idea simply because society finds the idea itself offensive or disagreeable." He concluded that preserving the fundamental right of freedom of expression, no matter how repugnant that expression may be, was more important than preserving the flag as a symbol of nationhood.

The dissenters were livid. Flag burning is not "speech," Chief Justice Rehnquist wrote, but rather "is the equivalent of an inarticulate grunt or roar" whose only purpose is "not to express any particular idea, but to antagonize others." Johnson was punished not for his ideas, said the dissenters, but for committing an act that is regarded as profoundly repulsive to the majority of citizens—and just as society has the right to legislate against offensive conduct like embezzlement and pollution, it has the right to legislate against flag burning.

The *Texas v. Johnson* decision provoked the House and Senate to pass condemnatory resolutions, and President George H. W. Bush supported a constitutional amendment outlawing flag desecration. Others in Congress supported an anti–flag burning statute. Those forces prevailed, resulting in the Flag Protection Act of 1989. Almost immediately, that law was challenged, and the Supreme Court ruled it to be unconstitutional on the same bases expressed in the *Texas v. Johnson* decision. Since that time, there have been repeated calls for a constitutional amendment but, to date, proponents have been unable to garner sufficient votes in the House and Senate to force the issue.

As for the line between conduct that is regarded as speech and protected under the First Amendment, and conduct that does not implicate the First Amendment, it is interesting to compare the Supreme Court's 1968 decision in *United States v. O'Brien*. In that case, O'Brien burned his draft card during an anti-war protest, and he was arrested under a federal law making the intentional destruction of a draft card a federal crime. O'Brien's draft card burning was plainly the same kind of political protest as Johnson's flag-burning, but this time the Supreme Court let the conviction stand. The difference, according to the Court, was that Congress had a legitimate interest in the preservation of draft cards in order to assure the efficient operation of the Selective Service System. So, while that element of O'Brien's conduct that was "speech" might be constitutionally protected, there was another element to his conduct that was not "speech" and could be punished.

33. New York Times Co. v. Sullivan

The Freedom to Criticize Public Officials and Public Figures 1964

Although the First Amendment protects "free speech," not everything that is said or written is defined as "speech" worthy of a First Amendment shield. Some examples have been discussed previously, like "fighting words" intended to incite immediate violence, or obscenity. Another example stems from the centuries-old common law of defamation: you cannot falsely call someone a thief or an incompetent in public, and then hide behind the First Amendment when you're sued for the damage you did to their reputation. Defamation law covers both false statements made in writing (libel) and false statements made in spoken form (slander). Either way, the law recognizes the right we all have to protect our good names.

At the same time, however, our democracy, like any democracy, depends on the ability of citizens to speak freely about their public officials without fear of reprisal. This is the essence of the First Amendment, and one of the key freedoms that distinguishes us from a dictatorship. But here's the difficult part: what happens if, in the course of speaking out about a public official, you inadvertently say something that turns out to be false? For instance, based on information you got from the town bookkeeper, you honestly think that the tax collector is embezzling tax money, and you say so at a public meeting. The tax collector is fired and his reputation is ruined. It turns out, however, that the bookkeeper was wrong, but you didn't know that at the time.

You certainly had a First Amendment right to speak out, but don't public officials have the right to protect their reputations, like anyone else? And if they do have the right to sue for libel and slander, what effect will that have on the willingness of citizens to freely speak their minds about important issues at the next public meeting?

In 1960, a group seeking, among other things, to raise funds for the legal defense of Martin Luther King Jr. ran a full-page ad in the *New York Times*. The ad included statements that the Montgomery, Alabama, police had engaged in serious acts of misconduct. As it turned out, the statements were false. L. B. Sullivan, the city official who oversaw the police department, brought a libel action against the *New York Times*, and a local jury awarded him the then-unprecedented sum of $500,000.

Is There a Right to Lie?

The *New York Times* appealed, claiming that the case violated crucial rights of free speech, and the Supreme Court agreed to hear the case. The issue was how the country should balance the First Amendment right to speak out about their public officials, against the right of those public officials to protect their reputations from false statements. In its decision, the Supreme Court spoke very clearly about which way that balance should tilt.

Justice Brennan wrote the Court's majority opinion. He began by stating the obvious: "Freedom of expression upon public questions is secured by the First Amendment." But he then went a remarkable step further and ruled that, contrary to the entrenched principles of defamation law, even false statements about public officials would from that time forward be protected by the First Amendment. Justice Brennan wanted to make sure that citizens could speak out about their public officials without having to look over their shoulders. As he put it, even false statements must be protected if this basic right of public discourse is to have the "breathing space" it needs to survive.

But Justice Brennan also set limits: only false statements about public officials *made in good faith* would be protected. No protection would be given to a false statement made with "malice"— that is, with the knowledge that it is false or, very important, with "reckless disregard" of whether it is false.

The *New York Times Co. v. Sullivan* limitation on defamation suits by public officials was extended in later cases to also include "public figures"—movie stars, people frequently in the media, and so on. The logic is that when you are in the public spotlight, the public should have a First Amendment right to talk about you in good faith, without fear of lawsuits.

The Real-World Impact of
New York Times Co. v. Sullivan

Picture a campaign for governor between Sam Smith and John Jones. Smith hires an investigator. The investigator tells Smith that he has evidence documenting that Jones uses cocaine. Smith immediately starts running attack ads, calling Jones the "Cocaine Candidate." Jones loses the election and his reputation is ruined. It turns out that the investigator's information was false—the drug user was a different John Jones, not the candidate. Jones sues Smith for libel. Smith defends by claiming that he placed the ads in good faith, based on the information provided by a professional investigator, and that, under the First Amendment, candidates in an election campaign are allowed to make mistakes. What more could he do?

Jones, however, wants to know whether Smith showed "reckless disregard" for whether or not the reports were false. As Justice Brennan explained, if Smith recklessly disregarded the truth, Smith could be liable to Jones. Did you make sure the investigator corroborated the sources? Did you personally interview any of the people who made the accusation? "John Jones" is a common name; did you do anything to make sure this was not a case of mistaken identity? Or did you just put on blinders because you wanted the information to be true?

The "reckless disregard" issue is the battleground on which these cases are usually fought. It is tough to prove that someone intentionally lied, and the question usually boils down to whether they cared enough about the truth to seek it out. Remember, in order to be liable for defamation of a public official, it takes more than just a disregard for whether a statement is false—it takes a *reckless* disregard, which is a much higher standard.

New York Times Co. v. Sullivan is there when a national news anchor reports a story on congressional misconduct; or when a local newspaper reporter attempts to expose a municipal conflict of interest; or when a citizen comes to a town meeting to complain that the mayor drinks too much; or when a business journal critiques the performance of a famous CEO; or when an Internet blog asserts that a rock star was lip-synching during a recent concert. It continues to define our rights of public discourse.

34. New York Times Co. v. United States

The Pentagon Papers Case: Balancing National Security Against the People's Right to Know 1971

What happens when a reporter obtains information about an important national issue of great interest to the American people, but the government believes that disclosure of the information would harm national security? Does national security trump a journalist's (or anyone else's) First Amendment right of free speech? If it does, how is it to be determined if the government's national security concerns are genuine, or are really just excuses to avoid political embarrassment?

In 1967, Secretary of Defense Robert S. McNamara commissioned a classified study to disentangle how the United States had become involved in the Vietnam War. The report took more than a year to complete and encompassed forty-seven volumes, with extensive documentary evidence. Later dubbed the "Pentagon Papers," it included evidence that the government had lied to and misled the American people, and that various presidents had overstepped their lawful powers.

Daniel Ellsberg was a Cambridge- and Harvard-educated economist who had served in the military, consulted with the government on key issues such as the Cuban missile crisis, and, having been identified as a rising intellectual resource, was asked to join the Defense Department in 1964 to work for McNamara. In this role, Ellsberg visited Vietnam and observed what he believed were substantial flaws in the development and implementation of United States policy. Ellsberg began to morph from an enthusiastic hawk to a very cynical dove.

From 1967 to 1969, Ellsberg, at McNamara's request, helped to compile the Pentagon Papers, and in the process Ellsberg further confirmed what he saw as rampant governmental deception and misconduct. At the height of his disillusionment, Ellsberg copied substantial portions of the Pentagon Papers and provided them to the press.

The *New York Times* began publishing excerpts from the Pentagon Papers, and the Nixon administration immediately filed a lawsuit, claiming that national security would be compromised if publication continued. Government lawyers successfully obtained an injunction to stop further publication—the first time the government had ever sought an injunction to stop a newspaper from publishing the news. The *New York Times* appealed to the Supreme Court; but in the interim, the *Washington Post* obtained a copy and began publication, resulting in another government lawsuit; the *Boston Globe* then began publication as well. The Supreme Court, recognizing the serious issues involved, expedited the usual procedures, immediately scheduled oral arguments, and just four days later issued its ruling.

Can the President Edit the Evening News?

Decades before, the Supreme Court had ruled that the First Amendment does not permit courts to order a "prior restraint" of free speech, except in the most unusual circumstances. In other words, courts can award damages if what is said or written constitutes libel or slander, and courts can send someone to jail if what is said or written constitutes a crime, but courts cannot, except in the most extraordinary cases, issue orders prohibiting the act of speaking or writing itself.

Owing to the speed with which the case found its way to the Court, the justices issued a joint, very brief opinion reiterating the law regarding prior restraints of speech, stating that the Nixon administration had "a heavy burden of showing justification" for the restraint on the publication of the Pentagon Papers, and concluding that it had not met that burden. The Pentagon Papers were published, and they fueled widespread and accelerating opposition to the Vietnam War, as well as increasing cynicism about government in general.

In addition to this brief statement, several justices of the Court used the case to publish their own lengthy and detailed opinions in which they expressed their views on freedom of the press, and in which they excoriated the government's attempt to stop the publication.

Some justices took the position, consistent with the rulings in some prior cases, that if the publication of certain information would clearly create a direct, immediate, and irreparable injury to the nation, a prior restraint could be issued. Those justices concurred in lifting the injunction against the Pentagon Papers, however, because they felt that the government had not come close to such a showing in the case before the Court.

Other justices, notably Justice Black and Justice Douglas, took the position that the government may *never* keep information from the public. Justice Black wrote, "In my view, it is unfortunate that some of my Brethren are apparently willing to hold that the publication of news may sometimes be enjoined. Such a holding would make a shambles of the First Amendment." He went on to describe the role the Founding Fathers had envisioned for the press: "The press was to serve the governed, not the governors. The Government's power to censor the press was abolished so that the press would remain forever free to censure the Government. . . . In revealing the workings of government that led to the Vietnam War, the newspapers nobly did precisely that which the Founders hoped and trusted they would do."

Freedom of the Press in a Post–9/11 World

In a post–9/11 world, the conflict between national security and the public's right to know, as exemplified by the Pentagon Papers case, has been heightened. This conflict raises many of the most difficult issues democracies face, and compelling arguments can be made in support of a variety of policy positions. The *New York Times*, for instance, was blessed by some and cursed by others for its exposure in 2005 of the government's previously secret program of domestic electronic eavesdropping, and a multitude of approaches has been suggested by congressmen, senators, and commentators of all parties and political leanings.

However the executive and legislative branches may choose to address these issues in the future, it is unlikely that their decisions will be the last word. The magnificence of a system of government like ours is this: when it works like it's supposed to work, whether the public's right to know has been properly respected by its elected officials is ultimately measured against the requirements of a Constitution that transcends whatever policy preferences may exist at any point in time. And the measuring is to be done by Supreme Court justices with no ax to grind other than the preservation of the core values of the Constitution itself.

CHAPTER 10

OLD LAWS AND NEW TECHNOLOGIES

"Invention is the mother of necessity."

—THORSTEIN VEBLEN,
ECONOMIST AND POLITICAL COMMENTATOR

About two hundred years ago, the cotton gin and the steam engine helped change an agricultural society into an industrial society. Mega-factories and a national economy soon followed, and families, workplaces, and governments were forever transformed. In response, a whole new body of laws emerged to address the never-imagined problems new technologies always bring with them. This is how jurisprudence evolves: with each new brainchild, there is always a need for new laws to help resolve new issues.

Yet the Constitution, an eighteenth-century document, remains the fundamental law of our land. How can it apply to twenty-first-century issues? Can an eighteenth-century prohibition against unreasonable searches be sensibly enforced against a twenty-first-century police force? Does the eighteenth-century concept of "free speech" have meaning to the twenty-first-century Internet?

And what happens if the Constitution turns out to be an ancient round peg that simply will not fit within a modern square hole?

A computer board; how will the Constitution adapt to modern technology?

35. MGM Studios Inc.
v. Grokster, Ltd.

Music, Movies, and the Internet 2005

Grokster, Ltd. was in the business of distributing free software that allows computer users to share and copy electronic files on a "peer-to-peer" basis—that is, directly from one computer to another computer without having to go through a central server. The Grokster software could be used to share any kind of computer file, but as Grokster well knew, the software was primarily used as a tool to infringe on copyrights—millions of times a month, Grokster users sent copyrighted materials to each other, such as music and video files. The effect was, basically, a high-tech, geometrically multiplied version of what would happen if one person buys a book and then makes thousands of copies and gives them away for free, in violation of the author or publisher's copyright.

To increase its user base, Grokster actively promoted its software as an easy and efficient way to exchange copyrighted music and video files, and even offered instructions to users who called the Grokster help line. Grokster was not paid by its users, but as the number of users increased, Grokster could generate more advertising revenue.

MGM (along with a group of other copyright holders) sued Grokster for copyright infringement. MGM sought an injunction to stop the use of the Grokster software, and also sought damages from Grokster for the copyright infringements committed by the computer users to whom Grokster distributed its software.

The "Guns Don't Kill People" Defense

Grokster had some solid defenses—and it won in the lower courts. There was no evidence that Grokster itself ever infringed on a copyright, and it was not contested that, for instance, students and business executives who wanted an efficient way to exchange word processing files or spreadsheets could and did use Grokster for completely legal purposes. Grokster contended that it could not be held responsible if users chose to employ its software for illegal purposes—the technological equivalent of the "guns don't kill people, people kill people" defense.

In fact, there was substantial legal precedent for Grokster's position. There was no basis in copyright law for holding someone liable for creating a product that others used to infringe copyrights. When Sony introduced its VCR, for example, movie studios sued, claiming they would be ruined because VCR users could unlawfully record and copy movies instead of going to theaters. The Supreme Court eventually heard the case, and ruled in favor of Sony. Yes, VCRs could be used to unlawfully copy movies, said the Court. But they were also capable of lawful use, and Sony could not be held responsible for the fact that some users might use them improperly.

When *MGM v. Grokster* got to the Supreme Court, Grokster made the same argument about its software that Sony had made about its VCR—but unlike Sony, Grokster lost. What was the difference?

In the *Grokster* case, the Supreme Court faced a situation in which it had to find a way to do something. If copyright protection means anything, owners of copyrighted materials, like music and video files, had to have a way to stop the blatant infringement that the peer-to-peer software enabled. In the past, copyright owners could sue those doing the infringing, but in the peer-to-peer world it was almost impossible to track down who was sending what computer file to whom. Billions of dollars were being lost.

Yet copyright law, as demonstrated by the Sony precedent, provided MGM with no rights against Grokster, since Grokster was not the one doing the infringing.

A Government of Men, and Not Laws?

Grokster is an excellent example of what happens when courts, armed only with laws rooted in the eighteenth century, confront twenty-first-century technology issues that the lawmakers never could have foreseen and that the laws were never meant to address. In reaching its decision, the Supreme Court exercised its supremacy, and did what it so frequently does when faced with such situations: it found a way to change the law so it could do what it felt had to be done.

The Supreme Court decided that even though Grokster made a product that, like the VCR, could be used for lawful purposes, Grokster had "induced" its customers to use its product for unlawful purposes, and Grokster should be held liable for that unlawful inducement. It was as if Grokster sold an electric screwdriver, but advertised and supported it as a means to pick locks and commit burglaries. The Supreme Court made it clear that "mere knowledge" of the fact that a product was being used unlawfully would not be enough to create liability. Sony, for instance, knew that some customers used VCRs unlawfully. But Sony marketed VCRs as a device to be used for lawful purposes, such as "time shifting"—recording a program so it could be viewed at another time. Grokster, on the other hand, energetically encouraged its users to take a product that could be used lawfully, and use it unlawfully; that was the difference between being liable and not being liable.

MGM v. Grokster will most certainly change the way Americans share music, video, and other copyrighted materials over the Internet. A concern raised by many commentators is whether it will also have a chilling effect on the development of new technologies that could be used for either lawful or unlawful purposes. The jury is (almost literally) still out on that fear. Apple originally marketed iTunes through its "Rip. Mix. Burn." slogan—an apparent invitation to copyright infringement—but has nevertheless won the approval of the recording industry. Portable hard drives that fit inside a wallet are perfect for copying MP3 music files from a friend's computer, but there is no apparent movement to ban these devices. The difference seems to lie in the fact that these products can be used primarily for lawful purposes, and the manufacturers are not, overtly or behind the scenes, promoting their use for unlawful purposes.

But what about the way in which this new body of law was created? A company like Grokster might convincingly argue that by departing from precedent in this way, the Supreme Court unfairly changed the rules in the middle of the game. What happened to the "government of laws, not men" concept? Didn't Grokster's owners, when they invested in the company, have a right to rely on the law as it was written at the time?

There are no easy answers. Ultimately, the law's job is to reflect society's views on what is fair and just. When faced with conduct that, while technically legal, violates society's sensibilities, the Supreme Court must make the difficult choice of either mechanically applying the law as it exists, or tweaking the law so that the results comport with established notions of justice. The Supreme Court often chooses the latter alternative: individuals and companies inevitably find the unforeseen cracks and loopholes in the law, and if the Supreme Court thinks the result is more than society should be required to tolerate, it does what it needs to do to seal the cracks and close the loopholes.

36. Kyllo v. United States

How Much Privacy Are You Entitled to in a High-Tech World? 2001

Unlike the implied right of privacy on which the *Griswold* and *Roe* cases discussed previously were based, there is an explicit right of privacy plainly expressed in the Fourth Amendment to the Constitution. That provision restricts the right of the government to snoop into the personal affairs of Americans through the admonition that the "right of the people to be secure in their persons, houses, papers, and effects, against unreasonable searches and seizures, shall not be violated." If the government wants to conduct a search, the Fourth Amendment mandates that it must go to a judge and obtain a warrant "upon probable cause, supported by Oath or affirmation, and particularly describing the place to be searched and the persons or things to be seized."

But how much privacy does the Fourth Amendment actually provide in a high-tech world, where the FBI and even the local police have electronic devices and computer capabilities that can do what the framers of the Constitution could not possibly have imagined?

Federal agents were suspicious that Danny Lee Kyllo was growing marijuana in his home. The agents secretly set up a thermal-imaging device outside the Kyllo home in order to determine if the heat emanating from the home was consistent with the high-intensity lamps typically used to nurture indoor marijuana plants. The scan showed that Kyllo's garage roof and a side wall were relatively hot compared to the rest of his home and were substantially warmer than neighboring homes. On the basis of that information, the agents obtained a warrant, searched Kyllo's home, found growing marijuana plants, and convicted Kyllo on a federal drug charge.

Kyllo argued that his conviction should be overturned because the government's use of the thermal-imaging device to detect what was going on inside his house was "an unreasonable search and seizure" that violated his rights under the Fourth Amendment. Still, how could that be? All the government did was monitor what was going on *outside* Kyllo's house.

Can You "Search" a House without Ever Going Inside?

Over many years, the Supreme Court has developed a body of rules that flesh out the meaning of the Fourth Amendment. At their core, these rules mandate that citizens are entitled to privacy within their homes, and that the only way the police can invade that privacy is by going to a judge, demonstrating the need to invade that privacy, and obtaining a warrant. There are some limited exceptions, such as true emergencies. But other than that, our homes are our castles, and the government's right to intrude into our homes requires a warrant.

Kyllo's situation presented another example of what happens when eighteenth-century laws meet twenty-first-century technology. What happens if, using the latest electronic and computer capabilities, the authorities can look inside your home without ever getting close to your front door, and without your even knowing they are in the neighborhood? Does the Fourth Amendment prohibit the government from analyzing what is happening outside a house in order to determine what is going on inside the house?

Kyllo lost his case in the lower courts, and the Supreme Court agreed to hear his appeal. Most commentators believe that since at least the 1990s, the Supreme Court has favored law enforcement authorities, and in the process has relaxed many of the rights afforded to those who

commit or are accused of committing crimes. Therefore, the presump-
tion was that Kyllo's argument would be viewed with disdain and that
the Supreme Court would use the case as a means to put another arrow
in law enforcement's quiver.

Privacy Trumps Technology

It did not turn out that way. Kyllo won. In the process, the Supreme
Court began the effort to set limits on "Big Brother" that will help to
further define twenty-first-century privacy rights.

The Supreme Court ruled that unless the government gets a warrant,
it cannot use a device that is not in general public use to effectively look
inside a private home from the outside: if the police would need a warrant to go into the house to find out what was going on inside, they must
get a warrant to accomplish the same result using high-tech devices
from outside the house. In years past, the Supreme Court had ruled that
the government can, without a warrant, use binoculars to look through
the windows of a house (or even fly overhead) to see what is in plain
view. But the *Kyllo* Court ruled that other than that, citizens have the
right to expect what's inside of their homes to remain private, and that
right of privacy is violated just as much by a police officer crawling
through a window as it is by the use of technology to accomplish the
same result. The message was clear: if the police want to see what's not
in plain view inside a private home, they need a warrant.

There are a myriad of technology-versus-privacy issues that the
Supreme Court has not yet had the opportunity to address, and *Kyllo*
may be a key indicator of the direction in which the Supreme Court
will head. For instance, the government has reportedly developed a
technology it calls "Magic Lantern," through which it can e-mail a
program to a suspect's computer and then monitor the suspect's com-

puter keystrokes. Isn't this a way to peer inside a home from outside the home, and wouldn't the logic of *Kyllo* require overenthusiastic government agents to first obtain a warrant?

What about homeowners who use wireless computer networks? Wireless network signals can be picked up from outside a home. Could local police who think you may be conducting illegal activities in your house set up on the public street outside your home, tap into your wireless network, monitor your e-mails, and search your hard drive?

In *Kyllo*, the Court stated its intent to protect fundamental rights against the end runs that new technologies can provide to government authorities. For citizens concerned about their rights of privacy, *Kyllo* is a first step in an important direction. An issue the Court will no doubt face in the future is whether deviations from that path should be permitted in the face of emerging law-enforcement challenges and national security issues.

37. United States v. American Library Association

The Internet, Free Speech, and the First Amendment 2003

The First Amendment's prohibition of laws "abridging the freedom of speech" is among our most cherished rights. As shown in some of the cases discussed previously, our traditions hold that free speech is a linchpin of democracy. Once government gets into the business of deciding what kinds of speech or written materials are appropriate, a very dangerous line has been crossed. Whatever social ill may result from allowing tasteless or repugnant expression is a price you pay for freedom.

But What About the Kids?

But consider this situation. To assist your thirteen-year-old son with his schoolwork, you buy him a notebook computer and arrange for a high-speed connection to the Internet. Later, you find out that he has been accessing pornographic Web sites. You can install filtering software on his computer, but those programs are anything but perfect; they can be expensive; and, besides, he's always going to have access to the Internet when he visits his friends. The Founding Fathers never envisioned anything like the Internet. Isn't there room in the First Amendment to protect children from Internet content they simply should not see?

In 1997, in the first Internet-related Supreme Court case, *Reno v. American Civil Liberties Union*, the Supreme Court considered the constitutionality of the federal Communications Decency Act (CDA). The CDA prohibited the transmission of any "indecent" or "patently offensive" messages or displays to a minor, or in a manner that is available to a minor. The question was whether the CDA violated the First Amendment, and the Supreme Court ruled that it did.

The Supreme Court reasoned that the Internet was a unique "marketplace of ideas," and, for the good of our democracy, it was entitled to the same broad First Amendment protections as books and other publications. The government was simply not entitled to "chill" free expression, even if that expression might be offensive to some, and yet the CDA would have precisely that effect. How would those persons responsible for Web sites dealing with, for instance, birth control practices, or homosexuality, or the legal issues involved in pornography know in advance if a court would ultimately find their materials to be "indecent" or "patently offensive," and how would they keep minors from accessing their materials without also barring access to adults? While it might be true that software could be devised so that Web sites could tag and filter potentially offensive content in a way that only adults could access, the Court decided that adults should not have to jump through technical hoops to read and view what they wanted.

The Court's ultimate conclusion was this: while minors need to be protected, that protection cannot be implemented in a way that burdens and compromises the First Amendment rights of adults, and the CDA, however laudable its purpose, went too far.

Now picture a situation in which you drop off your teenager at the local public library to do some research. After you leave, he heads for the library computer terminals and accesses Web sites that include pornographic materials. The library knows that kids might use its computers for this purpose. Shouldn't it block access to these sites?

But, on the other side of that coin, what about the First Amendment rights of adults who use those same computers to view whatever they want in a publicly funded library, free from government interference? Isn't a library the one place where you should be able to read anything you want without someone looking over your shoulder?

The Supreme Court confronted these questions in 2003, in the case of *United States v. American Library Association*. The case involved a challenge by the American Library Association to the constitutionality of a congressional statute that, for the purpose of protecting children, denied federal funding to libraries that refused to install filtering software that blocked obscene materials on all library computers.

The system envisioned by the statute would allow adults to have librarians unblock the computers while they were using them. But the reality was that adults would often be too embarrassed to make the request, fearing that they would be perceived as seeking to view pornography in the library when, in fact, that was not the case: the filtering software did not work very well and was a serious impediment to normal adult usage of the computers for research or casual reading. As a result, one justice wrote that, contrary to the very purpose of the First Amendment, the statute "prohibits reading without official consent." The American Library Association sued, it said, to protect what libraries are supposed to be.

Surprisingly to many, despite its decision in the *Reno* case, the Supreme Court ruled against the American Library Association's position and upheld the constitutionality of the statute. It concluded that so long as the library staff would freely unblock the filters without delay, the importance of protecting children outweighed the (theoretically) small burden on adult First Amendment rights occasioned by the requirement that they approach a librarian and ask for permission to read and view what they want. The implication of the ruling is that if, in practice, specific libraries fail to quickly accede to adult requests, those libraries may be required to remove the filters (and lose funding), but that was a bridge to be crossed later.

Defining the Future of the Internet

The *American Library Association* case is an important—some say scary—chink in the First Amendment armor in which the *Reno* case had cloaked the traditionally free-wheeling, anything-goes Internet. The issue is whether the case will be limited to its specific facts, or whether it signals a trend away from *Reno*, toward what many see as the slippery slope of Internet censorship. Given, for instance, the ubiquity of computer access that minors have in today's world, why shouldn't filters be required on all computers? And what if it turns out to be impractical to protect children from inappropriate Internet content through filtering devices that can be turned on and off? In the interest of protecting children, should Congress then attempt to regulate Internet content itself? And if it makes sense to regulate Internet content, what about blogs and e-mails? But if that's the tactic used, who will decide what Internet content should be filtered or restricted, and on what basis will those decisions be made?

There is no denying the breathtaking difficulty of such issues, and the Supreme Court has, although cautiously, entered the fray.

In 1998, in response to the *Reno* decision, Congress enacted the Child Online Protection Act (COPA). Like the CDA, COPA imposed fines and imprisonment for posting material "harmful to minors" on the World Wide Web, but it attempted to address the issues that caused the Supreme Court to find the CDA unconstitutional. COPA was, nevertheless, quickly ruled unconstitutional by lower courts, and after years of procedural wrangling the Supreme Court agreed, ruling in 2004, although by only a 5–4 majority, that COPA created the "potential for extraordinary harm and a serious chill upon protected speech."

But very significantly, rather than striking COPA from the statute books as it almost always does when it finds a law to be unconstitutional, the Supreme Court sent the case back to the lower court with orders that the lower court investigate whether the latest content-filtering technology could be used to achieve COPA's objectives. First Amendment advocates were alarmed, some to the point of panic, at the signals they saw in this result: they feared the prospect that filtering technologies would be found inadequate, and COPA, along with the right to censor Internet content, would on that basis be resurrected.

Years of litigation ensued, much of it focusing on the capabilities and limits of the evolving Internet-filtering technologies. Finally, in July 2008, in the case of *ACLU v. Mukasey*, the Court of Appeals for the Third Circuit (one of the courts that sits just below the Supreme Court in our federal judicial hierarchy) *again* ruled COPA unconstitutional. The Court based its ruling on the well-entrenched principle that even when there is a good reason to restrict free speech, the law must use the least restrictive means available to do so. Filtering programs, said the Court, may not be perfect, but they are effective enough—we can protect children without government censorship.

Undeterred, the Bush administration again sought to salvage COPA, and petitioned the Supreme Court to overrule the Third Circuit's conclusion. Filters were flawed, easily circumvented solutions, went the argument; minors had to be protected, and regulating Internet content was the only effective way to do it.

In January 2009, the Supreme Court refused to consider the Third Circuit's decision, effectively allowing COPA to die an unnatural death. Garnering the meaning from the Court's refusal to take action (as compared to instances where it accepts a case and then issues an opinion) can be risky business. It might mean that the Court felt that filtering technologies have advanced to the point where censorship is not necessary in order to protect minors. Or it might mean that the Court was not ready to address the issue, one way or the other, and chose to await another case on another day. The latter possibility will inevitably spur interest groups to bring new test cases highlighting the intersections between the First Amendment and objectionable Internet content.

The significance of the *American Library Association* case lies in the fact that it opened the door on the regulation of Internet content; the Internet is not sacrosanct, not untouchable, not beyond the reach of the law's efforts to serve countervailing interests. Whether the case represents the outer limit of permissible Internet regulation, or just a first step, will be defined by future cases. The decisions made in those cases will ultimately define much of the face and function of the Internet itself, and the effect of those precedents will ripple in unforeseeable ways through the myriad other technologies and innovations that so dominate our society.

CHAPTER 11

PRESIDENT OBAMA AND THE SUPREME COURT: WHAT DOES THE FUTURE HOLD?

*"It is confidence in the men and women who administer the judicial
system that is the true backbone of the rule of law."*

—JUSTICE JOHN PAUL STEVENS

In fundamental respects, the Constitution does not mean what it
says. It means what the Supreme Court says it means. Or, more
particularly, it means what five Supreme Court justices say it means at
any particular time.

When a president has the opportunity to select a candidate for the
Supreme Court, pundits, politicians, and interest groups unfailingly
demand a nominee who will "interpret the law as written" rather than
"legislating from the bench" or "making policy." It's become a patriotic
mantra, an understandable plea against judicial extremism. But when
it comes to the Supreme Court, these sorts of directives, unless properly
understood, can be naïve and nonsensical distractions that misdirect
the social debate a Supreme Court nomination should provoke.

If we're going to live by our Constitution, someone's got to tell us
what it means in practice and as applied to unanticipated situations and
ever-changing circumstances. The Constitution does not lay out the
answers; it depends on the Supreme Court to find the answers within

President Obama signs the guest book during his January 14, 2009 visit to the Supreme Court, as
Chief Justice John Roberts Jr. looks on.

its broadly stated, sometimes obtuse precepts, and to change previous answers when our social experience demands it. A Supreme Court justice fearful of "legislating from the bench" or "making policy" would have floundered when asked to determine if citizens can sue the government when their rights are violated, or if an individual can be jailed for burning the flag in an anti-war protest, or if school districts can require students to recite prayers — there is nothing in the Constitution that directly answers those questions. A Supreme Court justice who resolved only to "interpret the law as written" would have never overruled *Plessy v. Ferguson* in favor of *Brown v. Board of Education* — the judicial branch, after all, is supposed to respect established precedent rather than changing laws to suit individual preferences.

This book is all about the cases where, thankfully, the Supreme Court — sometimes cheered by the left, sometimes cheered by the right — undertook the daunting task of interpreting the Constitution's often-vague and arcane language (as opposed to interpreting "the law as written") in order to define the laws and policies that make us who we are. That doesn't mean the Supreme Court should engage in unbounded forays into social engineering based on personal agendas. That doesn't mean the Supreme Court always comes up with a decision that stands the test of time. But it does mean that in a constitutional democracy we need constitutional answers, and it's up to the Supreme Court to provide them. The Supreme Court tells us, for instance, how far the government can go in restricting campaign contributions, gun ownership and free speech; what are the limits on presidential power; just how free our system of free enterprise shall be; where the lines must be drawn between church and state; how can we distinguish between affirmative action and race discrimination; and the extent to which the law can limit our personal choices, such as abortion or suicide.

In considering candidates for the Supreme Court, the question is not whether they should make law and policy. Of course they should.

That's their job. The question is what kind and quality of law and policy they are likely to make; how honestly and objectively they will perform their duties; what personal attributes and experiences will influence their decisions; and whether the country will be better or worse for their efforts.

The retirement of Justice Souter in 2009 gave President Obama the opportunity to nominate his first Supreme Court candidate, Sonia Sotomayor; very likely, it will not be his last opportunity. We live in unique and unusual times, domestically and internationally, and his choices could alter the social, cultural, and political landscape of America for decades. What sort of Supreme Court does President Obama seek? And what difference will it make to you, your family, your job, and your country?

A Tenuous Balance of Power

For several years, the Supreme Court has existed in a delicate equilibrium, comprised of four judicial and political "liberals"; four judicial and political "conservatives"; and Justice Kennedy, the usual swing vote, who sometimes sides with the "liberals" but more often tilts toward the "conservatives." (The meaning of the "liberal" and "conservative" labels as used in these contexts is explained later.)

Not all issues divide the Court, and Chief Justice Roberts has made it a priority to tamp down ideological divisiveness. But in recent years the cases most Americans find most important have been characterized by 5–4 votes: gun rights, abortion, racial preferences, the war on terror, campaign finance reform, and many more. A shift in the Court's equilibrium could easily result in monumental changes; so much of what defines America hangs in this literal balance, for better or worse, depending on your point of view.

The prospect of a seismic change in existing Supreme Court precedent is real.

Two of the justices on the liberal side of the equation could easily depart in the next few years. Justice Stevens was born in 1920. Justice Ginsburg was born in 1933 and has been treated for cancer. None of the conservative justices, on the other hand, show any sign of leaving the bench in the foreseeable future. Chief Justice Roberts, Justice Alito and Justice Thomas are just entering their judicial prime, having been born in 1955, 1950, and 1948, respectively. Justices Scalia and Kennedy were born in 1936, and they remain energetic and ambitious.

Thus, the justices most likely to leave the Court all sit on the liberal side. For the reasons explained later in this chapter, and as demonstrated by his Sotomayor selection, if the opportunity to replace one or more sitting justices arises, President Obama will choose new justices with similar liberal predispositions. *If* his choices hold true to these predispositions, and *if* no conservative justices depart in the meanwhile, and *if* Justice Kennedy stays in the jurisprudential middle, the current equilibrium will *probably* remain intact.

But these are big, unknowable ifs. The attempt to predict how human beings will behave over time and in unforeseen circumstances is always risky business—and that renders the appointment of *any* new justice replete with uncertainties.

For one thing, Supreme Court justices don't always end up being what those who appointed them thought they would be—a lifetime appointment to a court answerable to no other court, coupled with the power to change society, has its effects. As Harry Truman once put it, "Whenever you put a man on the Supreme Court, he ceases to be your friend." If the history of Supreme Court justices teaches us anything, it's that a justice's past is not always a justice's prologue. A putative liberal justice could, as time goes by, end up allying more with the conservative than the liberal wing of the Court, and if that happens, the conservatives would have a five-justice majority. Many legal scholars believe that the existing Court is already the most conservative Court in decades, and a working conservative majority would allow it to finish the job.

Unexpected resignations from the Court also happen. Justice Souter made no secret of his desire to leave, but he knew that if he left during the Bush administration he would be replaced by a conservative justice, which would create a conservative majority on the Court. It came as no surprise that he resigned only months after the election of a president he knew would strive to maintain the current liberal/conservative balance. But the recent departures of Justice O'Connor and Chief Justice Rehnquist were not anticipated—both wanted to remain on the Court. Justice O'Connor left for family reasons, and Chief Justice Rehnquist left for health reasons. If a sitting conservative justice were to step down during the Obama administration (and it is worth noting that Justice Scalia will reach his eightieth birthday in an Obama second term) and is replaced with a liberal justice, the liberal wing could establish a five-justice majority, and along with it the ability to decide the important issues the Court will confront in coming years, coupled with the ability to reverse existing conservative precedents.

Justice Kennedy has staked out a more-or-less middle ground, but a slight shift in either direction could portend momentous significance for future cases. The insertion of a new justice into the Supreme Court dynamic has caused such shifts in the past—Supreme Court justices are always influenced by other Supreme Court justices, and there is no way to foretell how Justice Kennedy might be influenced by the personalities and persuasiveness of President Obama's appointments.

As, hopefully, the prior chapters have made clear, who sits on the Supreme Court can be as important as who sits in the White House. It matters, especially now, when a host of crucial issues seem poised for arrival on the Supreme Court's docket.

Why Don't Supreme Court Justices Just Stick to What the Constitution Says?

Why should the idiosyncrasies of a Supreme Court justice matter? We've got a Constitution. It says what it says; if it's in the strike zone, it should be called a strike. Why are there such differences among individual justices?

The Constitution establishes the mechanics of how the nation is to be assembled and operated in a clear and definitive way—it delineates the branches of government and their respective responsibilities, it sets certain boundaries between federal versus state powers, it describes how and when we are to elect presidents and congressional representatives, and so on.

But the Constitution is much more than a national owner's manual.

Parents understand the need to equip their children with more than a set of instructions that will allow them to survive. Parents struggle to define and instill in their children an array of key values that will help them lead satisfying, productive, and ethical lives, and to which they can turn for guidance. By their nature, however, such values can be expressed only through broad precepts that must be interpreted and applied by the child as unforeseeable conundrums and challenges arise in the future. The struggle of every parent is to be specific enough to provide a meaningful foundation that can help a child through the most important aspects of life, while at the same time being general enough to encompass the unknowns a child will inevitably face after leaving the nest.

Those who gave birth to our nation understood this as they struggled, like parents, to guide the nation they created through an unknowable future. Once they settled on the nation's structure, they defined the values to which the nation would adhere—certain foundational lines that could not be crossed, largely for the purpose of making certain that the government they created would serve, and not dominate, the governed. But at the same time, they knew that, given the uncertainties of the future, they could only define so much. Some other process by which the nation's values would evolve within the constitutional boundaries they set would have to arise from the executive/legislative/judicial structure they designed.

Enter the Supreme Court . . .

For example, the Constitution's framers knew that their forebears had fled from state-sponsored religious intolerance. They therefore mandated in the First Amendment that the government cannot interfere with the "free exercise" of religion, and it cannot "make laws respecting an establishment of religion." That dictate established a general baseline. But when the specific issue of whether mandatory school prayer violated those constitutional precepts arose, it fell to the then-sitting Supreme Court justices to pick up where the Constitution left off. Six of those justices concluded that mandatory school prayer did violate the First Amendment, and it was outlawed. The Constitution did not address the issue, and so the Constitution came to mean what six justices said it means. Many lower court judges and legal scholars disagreed with the decision, and still do—to them, mandatory school prayer is no more than an affirming nod to how the framers of the Constitution themselves commenced the very conclaves at which they wrote the First Amendment. If just two of those lower court judges or legal scholars had been appointed to the Supreme Court instead of those who made the decision, the school prayer cases would have been decided in a very different way.

The Constitution's framers also forbade the government from making laws that abridge freedom of speech. But does that mean that the

Constitution protects flag burning and obscenity? The framers mandated that our lives, liberty, and property cannot be compromised by those in power without due process of law. But does that mean that foreign nationals suspected of terrorism cannot be held overseas, as the military thinks best, unless they are given a full hearing? The framers made certain that those charged with a crime have the right to a public trial by an impartial jury and the right to confront and rebut the witnesses and evidence that may be used to convict them. But does that mean that the taxpayers have to foot the bill to pay for a lawyer for everyone who cannot afford one? The framers revolutionized the nature of government itself and affirmed that in our country, all persons are entitled to the equal protection of the laws. But does equal treatment necessarily mean that white people and black people have to go to the same schools?

The Constitution does not answer these issues. The real world answer is this: "yes, if a majority of justices who happen to be sitting on the Supreme Court when the issue is raised say so." Against this background, the 5–4 decisions discussed in the preceding chapters illuminate how exceptionally important a single justice can be. This is as discomforting as it is unavoidable. Yes, we're a nation of laws, not men; but men make the laws.

Activists, Textualists, Strict Constructionists, Liberals, Conservatives . . .

Given that individual Supreme Court justices have so much influence over our lives, what kind of justices do we want sitting on the Court?

The Constitution's eighteenth-century framers could not have envisioned our twenty-first-century issues and the questions and conflicts that flow from them: industrialization, globalization, complex financial systems, the Internet, climate change, computers, terrorism, the modern workplace, and so on. Sometimes the Constitution's precepts are easily adaptable. For instance, many of the free speech issues that arise from the use of the twenty-first-century Internet are conceptually identical to the free speech issues that arose from the use of an eighteenth-century soapbox. But sometimes the gaps are too large, and what the Constitution had to say then does not match up in an obvious way with the problems that need to be solved now.

Some justices take a "textualist" approach to this challenge. Look at the Constitution's words first. If that would lead to an absurd result, look at the context and history of the Constitution in order to derive the intent of those who drafted it . . . and stop there. If that doesn't illuminate a Constitutional solution, accept the fact that the Constitution was not meant as a cure-all, and that there are some issues that the Supreme Court should leave for others to resolve, such as the Congress and state governments.

Other justices believe that the Constitution should be given a broader reach. Yes, look closely at the words and the intent of the Constitution's framers . . . but *do not* stop there. They believe that those who drafted the Constitution intended its purposefully vague language and concepts to be interpreted within modern contexts—as times change, so should this "living Constitution." Otherwise, our founding document will ultimately be interpreted into irrelevancy.

Justices who trend toward the first camp are often referred to as judicial "conservatives." Justices who trend toward the second camp are often referred to as judicial "liberals." Conservatives often view liberals as situational ethicists, willing to make decisions on the basis of their own views or whatever happens to be the popular social or political view of the time, rather than abiding by the Constitution as truly conceived. Liberals often view conservatives as endorsing a Constitutional perspective that departs from common sense, and that makes the Constitution a historical document with limited utility—something those who wrote the Constitution never intended.

Conservatives are sometimes referred to, a bit pejoratively (and usually inaccurately), as "strict constructionists." Liberals are sometimes referred to, very pejoratively (and usually inaccurately), as "judicial activists."

Consider the *Griswold* case, in which the Supreme Court ruled that state laws prohibiting contraception are unconstitutional because they impinge upon an implicit constitutional right of privacy. Contraception is an issue about as far from the world of those who wrote the Constitution as one might envision, and there is no wording in the Constitution that speaks directly to that issue, or to the existence of a general right of privacy.

Therefore, conservatives argue that while these laws are undeniably absurd, they are not unconstitutional, because the Constitution does not deal with laws of this type, one way or the other. It's one thing for the Supreme Court to interpret the reach and meaning of the free exercise clause or the commerce clause and to make law on that basis; it's something much different to delve into areas where the Constitution is silent, where its language simply has no apparent relevance or application, and in those situations conservatives believe the Supreme Court ought to back off and let each state do as it will. We should limit ourselves to a fair reading of the words of the Constitution and the intent of those who wrote it, and no more. Otherwise, we enter the realm of creating, not just interpreting, the Constitution.

That's an abdication of our responsibility, say the liberals. One of the Constitution's building blocks is protecting people from unnecessary government intrusion. The Constitution may not tell us in so many words that people have a right to keep the government out of their marital lives, but it's our job to carry out the Constitution's intent. If we don't, say the liberals, the Constitution itself is minimized, and the people lose the protections it's supposed to provide.

Does Political Philosophy Matter More than Judicial Philosophy?

But what *really* drives judicial decision-making, particularly on the big issues, the ones that affect the lives of most Americans? Is it a disciplined adherence to a philosophy of constitutional interpretation? Do "judicial liberals" and "judicial conservatives" really stick to their philosophical notions, if doing so will produce what they think to be the wrong result? Or, when the time comes for signing off on truly important decisions, do Supreme Court justices depend more on their *political* philosophies as opposed to their *judicial* philosophies?

Take *Bush v. Gore*. Most legal scholars agree that a conservative judicial philosophy would have dictated a hands-off approach—there's nothing in the Constitution that militates in favor of interfering with a state's determinations respecting its election methods, which are typically left to state discretion. Yet the judicial conservatives on the Court voted to intervene in Florida's procedures and stop the recount, effectively awarding the presidency to George W. Bush—judicial conservatives seemingly engaged in judicial activism. The judicial liberals on the Court took a conservative, hands-off approach and voted to let Florida's recount proceed. When all was said and done, judicial philosophies took a back seat. But the justices who stopped the recount and put an ostensibly conservative President Bush in the White House were plainly the Court's more politically conservative justices, and those whose decision would have favored an ostensibly liberal Al Gore were the Court's more politically liberal justices. Political predilections seemingly trumped judicial predilections.

Or take the *Davis v. FEC* case, involving campaign finance reform. The campaign finance reform provisions at issue were generally opposed by political conservatives and generally favored by political liberals. Not coincidentally, the four most politically conservative justices—Roberts, Alito, Scalia, and Thomas, joined by Kennedy— found the provisions unconstitutional, and the four most politically liberal justices—Stevens, Souter, Ginsburg, and Breyer—found the provisions to be constitutionally valid. It was the judicial conservatives who took an activist stance and overruled legislation passed by the country's elected representatives and signed by the president, all of whom had concluded that the influence of money in the political process must be blunted. It was the judicial liberals who, contrary to their supposed nature, deferred to the congressional judgment that the pernicious influence of money on the electoral process required that action be taken. The "activist" liberals chided their conservative colleagues for concocting constitutional problems for the purpose of substituting their policy judgments for those of the country's elected legislators.

Or take the *District of Columbia v. Heller* "right to bear arms" case. Gun rights are generally supported by political conservatives; gun control is generally supported by political liberals. The Court's political conservatives (Roberts, Alito, Scalia, and Thomas, joined by Kennedy) interpreted the Constitution to include an individual right to bear arms; the Court's political liberals (Stevens, Souter, Ginsburg, and Breyer) found there to be no such constitutional right. Each side claimed that objective, independent scholarship backed their point of view, which just so happened to coincide with their political perspective.

Or take the *Boumediene v. Bush* case, involving the Guantanamo detainees. Political liberals generally opposed the Bush administration's Guantanamo policy, arguing that the executive branch does not have the authority to avoid the rule of law through such territorial machinations. Political conservatives generally supported the Bush administration's Guantanamo policy, arguing that unelected and unschooled judges ought not to interfere in wartime strategies and foreign policy issues. Justices Stevens, Souter, Ginsburg, and Breyer, the Court's politically liberal wing, this time joined by Justice Kennedy, all found the Bush administration's actions to be unconstitutional. Justices Roberts, Alito, Scalia, and Thomas, the Court's politically conservative bloc, all dissented.

Here's the point: Supreme Court justices are human. They, like everyone else, are products of their backgrounds. They care. They have opinions. They want to do the right thing, as they see it, particularly on the issues that have substantial and widespread impact. Neither a belief that the Constitution should be read and applied narrowly nor a belief that the Constitution should be read and applied broadly will always stand in the way of a justice who sees the lawful, good faith opportunity to right what is perceived as a serious wrong.

Much has been made of President Obama's stated preference, as reflected in the Sotomayor nomination, for Supreme Court justices with "empathy" for those who seek to overcome disadvantages, for David as opposed to Goliath. And there are reasonable bases on which those of differing perspectives can find fault with his view. But it is not accurate to characterize a justice with these penchants, or any other penchants, as one who will necessarily disregard the law or act improperly. Supreme Court justices routinely face questions to which there is no "right" answer, and a future justice's life experience will dictate what is "right" to that justice. During his confirmation hearing, senators questioned whether, given his personal history, now-Chief Justice Roberts could ever understand and identify with the "little guy." As it has turned out, during his tenure to this point, in virtually every case involving a confrontation between business and government on the one hand, and an individual claiming unlawful or unfair treatment on the other, Chief Justice Roberts has ruled in favor of business and government. That does not make him wrong, but it does bespeak a point of view—one that, like the opposite point of view, a Supreme Court justice is fully entitled to lawfully adopt and promote.

The reality is that a justice who is criticized for being a "strict constructionist" is usually a justice who failed to overturn a law or a decision that you thought was wrong; and a justice who is criticized for being a "judicial activist" is usually a justice who overturned a law or a decision that you thought was right.

Is Another Warren Court on the Way?

Barack Obama was the president of the *Harvard Law Review* and a professor of constitutional law at the University of Chicago Law School from 1992 until his election to the Senate in 2004. He has studied the Constitution, Supreme Court precedent, each of the sitting justices, and how significantly Supreme Court jurisprudence will be affected by any appointments he makes. Based on this expertise, he has a clear view of who he thinks should sit on the Court, and he does not need surrogates to explain and assess the qualifications of potential candidates—he has or can easily obtain a detailed awareness of the views, predilections, and writings of most of the men and women likely to be considered.

It is clear from his statements and writings that President Obama will use his expertise to seek judicial liberals; in his 2006 book, *The Audacity of Hope*, he wrote that the Constitution is "not a static but rather a living document, and must be read in the context of an ever-changing world." During the September 2005 confirmation hearings for Chief Justice Roberts, then-Senator Obama stressed the empathy factors that he continued to express when he made his Sotomayor nomination. He argued that while an analysis of phraseology and precedent can provide the basis on which to resolve most cases, there are "truly difficult" cases that are not so easily analyzed, and those cases "can only be determined on the basis of one's deepest values, one's core concerns, one's broader perspectives on how the world works, and the depth and breadth of one's empathy." During a pre-election interview, he reiterated the point, stating that we "need somebody who's got the heart, the empathy, to recognize what it's like to be a young teenage mom. The empathy to understand what it's like to be poor, or African-American, or gay, or disabled, or old. And that's the criteria by which I'm going to be selecting my judges."

This is, plainly, a viewpoint in keeping with the traditions of judicial liberalism.

What will be the political stance of the justices President Obama will favor? In the political context, the term "liberal" as applied to a Supreme Court justice generally means that the justice focuses on individual rights, particularly when the individual is relatively power-less, needs help, or is endangered by business or government, and that the justice will interpret the Constitution in a modern context to see if there is a justifiable basis through which to get the job done. President Obama plainly favors justices who are politically liberal. He voted against the confirmation of Justice Alito because, he said, his lower court judicial record showed "extraordinarily consistent support for the powerful against the powerless" and a bias toward "an overreaching federal government against individual rights and liberties."

The real question is just *how* judicially and politically liberal President Obama's appointees will be, recognizing the substantial difference between far-left liberals and centrist liberals, and what that will likely mean in real world terms. By all indications, President Obama's actions are and will likely remain substantially less liberal than many of his words.

The Warren Court of the 1950s and 1960s defined far-left judicial and political liberalism. It draws its name from Chief Justice Earl Warren who, when appointed in 1953 by President Eisenhower, was thought to be an establishment-oriented, "middle-of-the-road" former governor who would keep the Supreme Court in the background. It did not turn out that way, and when presidents and senators talk about the importance of carefully vetting Supreme Court candidates, Earl Warren is most often put forth as the reason why.

Warren, along with full-fledged iconic liberals like Justices William O. Douglas and William J. Brennan, led a precedent-busting civil rights revolution that changed the functional meaning of the Constitution and the social and political face of the country. The Warren Court issued opinions that eliminated segregation and enforced desegregation orders, outlawed race-based electoral redistricting, mandated "the one man, one vote" requirement in congressional districts, applied the Fifth Amendment rule against self-incrimination to state courts, created the "exclusionary rule" barring unlawfully obtained evidence from criminal cases, banned mandatory school prayer and Bible reading in public schools, upheld the right to assemble for lawful protests at state buildings, established the right of indigents to counsel in criminal cases, established the right of suspects to remain silent, mandated "Miranda" warnings, defined the standards under which obscene material could and could not be criminalized, protected the NAACP from state efforts to ban its activities, banned mandatory loyalty oaths, established the right of the federal government to use the Commerce Clause to fight discrimination, invalidated laws criminalizing cohabitation or marriage by interracial couples, defined the right of conscientious objector status, protected news organizations from libel status in the absence of recklessness, protected rights of free association among individuals, extended search and seizure protections to wiretaps, invalidated laws against the teaching of evolution in public schools, defined the free speech rights of students in public schools, established a constitutional right to travel, outlawed anti-contraception status on right of privacy grounds, outlawed poll taxes . . . and so on.

Is the Warren Court President Obama's model? He has spoken of Chief Justice Warren in glowing terms, stating that he "had the wisdom to recognize that segregation was wrong less because of precise socio-logical effects and more so because it was immoral and stigmatized blacks." In a pre-election interview with CNN's Wolf Blitzer in May 2008, he explained the humanistic, Warren Court–like approach to the law he looks for in a judicial candidate:

> What you're looking for is somebody who is going to apply the law where it's clear. Now, there's gonna be those five percent of cases or one percent of cases where the law isn't clear. And the judge has to then bring in his or her own perspectives, his ethics, his or her moral bearings—and, in those circumstances, what I do want is a judge who is sympathetic enough to those who are on the outside, those who are vulnerable, those who are powerless, those who can't have access to political power and as a conse-quence can't protect themselves from being dealt with sometimes unfairly. The courts become a refuge for justice. That's been its historic role. That was its role in *Brown v. Board of Education.*

These are sentiments that Chief Justice Warren would have gladly endorsed: in this construct, Supreme Court justices must do more, *much* more, than search for the Constitution's original meaning and intent; rather, they must be sympathetic, conscience-driven social activ-ists who look at the Constitution as a document intended to advance the country's highest and best ideals, especially in regard to those who need the most help.

But whatever his views may be, President Obama functions in a world of political realities, and he knows it. Even if he were inclined to seek a new Warren Court (which is by no means clear), the political realities President Obama now faces preclude him from appointing justices whose liberalism would extend anywhere close to the Warren Court. Pre-election rhetoric matters little at this point; the Oval Office looks much different from the inside than it does from the outside. Job one is quelling the partisanship and building the alliances required to deal with the screaming domestic and international crises at hand, and his appointment of a far left (or, for that matter, far right) Supreme Court candidate would create the kind of political and media firestorm that stops alliance-building in its tracks. Given the substantial Democratic majority in the Senate, which has to approve his choice, President Obama could probably get away with appointing a far-left candidate were he inclined to do so. But he won't, just as he did not appoint cabinet members who were likely to inflame partisan divisions. The art of politics, which he well understands, is accomplishing the most while offending the least.

The Sotomayor nomination makes this plain. As of this writing in June 2009, Sotomayor has not withstood the confirmation process but, no matter, Obama's choice indicates where along the liberal/conservative continuum he is aiming. *The Wall Street Journal* opined that "[s]he does not appear to be as liberal or left-wing as others who could have been picked."[1]

The *Journal* editorialized that her decisions, were anything but far left and "put her within the mainstream of Democratic judicial appointees," it pointed out that her record "shows her occasional siding with corporate defendants or diverting from a standard liberal position," and it quoted a corporate lawyer who reassured that "[t]here is no reason for the business community to be concerned" about Sotomayor.[2]

Early criticisms of the Sotomayor nomination expressed the fear that she would unfairly favor those who made race discrimination claims. SCOTUSblog, a highly respected source of Supreme Court news and analysis, studied the ninety-six race-related decisions in which Judge

1. *The Wall Street Journal*, May 29, 2009.
2. *The Wall Street Journal*, May 27, 2009.

Sotomayor was involved on the Court of Appeals, and found that she rejected discrimination claims on roughly an 8 to 1 ratio.[3]

Soft on crime? A McLatchy Newspapers review of her criminal law record concluded that while on the Court of Appeals, Judge Sotomayor sided with the government sixty-five times and prisoners and defendants twenty-five times.[4]

President Obama seeks justices who favor the "living Constitution" and empathetic viewpoint he has so many times expressed, but he will not have to aim far left, or anywhere close to the Warren Court, to find that kind of justice. His goal will be to maintain nothing less than the current Supreme Court equilibrium in the short run and, if given the opportunity, to move the Court a notch or two to the left of Justice Kennedy, its current center. A Sotomayor-type appointment serves his judicial and political purposes, and more of essentially the same (perhaps a bit more left-leaning depending on future electoral realities) can be expected in the event of additional vacancies—judicially and politically liberal, but not so much so as to make an easy and obvious target for conservative objectors.

How Will All of This Affect Our Lives?

So, when all is said and done, if any of the present liberal justices should leave the bench during the Obama administration, the Supreme Court will probably (though not certainly) stay within a general range of where it is—equally divided between liberals and conservatives with Justice Kennedy, who tilts toward the conservative viewpoint, in the

3. SCOTUSblog, May 29, 2009.
4. *Miami Herald*, May 29, 2009.

middle. If any of the conservative justices leave the bench, a five-justice liberal majority could form, though it is likely that at least two members of this new liberal coalition, Justice Breyer and the new appointee, would hold views closer to the center. In that scenario, Justice Breyer could emerge as the new "swing vote" justice, which would make it more likely that the 5–4 votes that have previously favored the conservative viewpoint would now favor the liberal viewpoint.

Having said all that, those who dare to suppose how individual justices, let alone the entire Court, will decide the defining issues of our time over the next ten or so years are quite like the television meteorologists who appear on Monday to predict what the weather will be for a picnic next Sunday. Yes, existing patterns can be identified and past history provides solid data on the trends that usually result from those patterns. But in both contexts, it's difficult to foresee the occasional winds of change—there are too many variables to account for. In many areas of law, the "liberal" and "conservative" labels don't lead to a predictable approach. And above all else, Supreme Court justices are people. They are influenced by the particular facts of the cases before them, by each other, by the times in which they live, and by their ever-evolving perspectives and points of view.

Still, on many issues, it remains possible to make some educated forecasts. So here goes, as of June 2009, with the Court equally balanced among liberals and conservatives and before the Sotomayor confirmation (but with the assumption that, no matter what, a similarly disposed candidate will fill the Souter vacancy).

ABORTION. The liberal side of the Court generally (and with some individual variations) supports abortion rights and disdains many of the restrictions that have been layered on top of *Roe v. Wade*. They don't have the votes to overturn those restrictions.

The conservative members of the Court would be very tempted to overturn *Roe* if they could. They don't have the votes to get there.

Justice Kennedy sits in the middle. He is personally opposed to abortion, but has previously voted in favor of preserving the right of abortion as first set forth in *Roe v. Wade*, to the chagrin of those who had foreseen him as a consistently conservative voice. However, in *Gonzales v. Carhart*, the case that upheld the legality of the ban on partial-birth abortions, Justice Kennedy not only sided with the majority; he wrote the majority opinion. This signals that Justice Kennedy, the current pivot point, would not overturn *Roe*, but would be willing to support federal or state legislation that restricts it.

The question for the immediate future is how far Justice Kennedy would allow those restrictions to go. Many Supreme Court justices, including Justice Kennedy, are loath to flout public opinion or cause public outcry. The likely answer is that he may support the constitutionality of restrictions such as public funding cuts and regulations affecting minors, but will not support any decision that substantially compromises the right of a woman to obtain an abortion.

What would happen if one of the current justices left the Court?

President Obama has been a staunch supporter of abortion rights, and was a cosponsor of a Senate bill that invalidated any federal or state interference with a woman's effort to obtain an abortion. It is safe to assume that he will choose justices of like mind. Senator McCain had vowed to appoint justices who were likely to vote in favor of overturning *Roe*, so the 2008 election was a turning point on the abortion issue.

If, therefore, another liberal justice leaves, things will most likely stay where they are—the departing justice would be replaced with another justice supportive of abortion rights. But if President Obama has the opportunity to replace one of the conservative members of the Court, the landscape will change: at that point, there would likely be a five-justice majority that supports abortion rights. That would not only put a stop to further restrictions on abortions, it might also result in a significant rollback of existing restrictions.

SAME-SEX MARRIAGE. Within the current Court, Justice Kennedy again appears to be the fulcrum on this issue, having led the way toward an expansion of constitutional rights pertaining to sexual orientation—again angering conservatives who thought him to be staunchly in the conservative camp. He wrote the opinion in the 1996 case, *Romer v. Evans*, that invalidated a provision in the Colorado constitution that sought to ban any legislation that would protect homosexuals from discrimination. He wrote the Court's 2003 opinion in *Lawrence v. Texas*, which invalidated laws that criminalized homosexual sodomy.

In *Lawrence*, Justice Kennedy did not directly discuss same-sex marriage, but his stated rationale could easily be applied to the issue: "Our laws and tradition afford constitutional protection to personal decisions relating to marriage, procreation, contraception, family relationships, child rearing, and education," he said, and the Constitution requires respect "for the autonomy of the person in making these choices." He went one step further, stating, "[p]ersons in a homosexual relationship may seek autonomy for these purposes, just as heterosexual persons do."

Yet, at the same time, Justice Kennedy voted with the conservatives and against his liberal colleagues in the *Boy Scouts v. Dale* case, explained in a prior chapter. This is not inconsistent with a view that protects what gays choose to do in their private lives, but it is indicative of a view that will restrict the constitutional reach of gay rights more than the liberal wing of the Court would favor.

Justice Scalia wrote, in his dissenting opinion in *Lawrence*, that the decision "leaves on pretty shaky grounds state laws limiting marriage to opposite-sex couples." Many constitutional law scholars agree that the logic of *Lawrence* makes bans on same-sex marriage constitutionally suspect. But post-*Lawrence* constitutional challenges to restrictions on same-sex marriage have been filed, and the Supreme Court has refused to hear them, indicating that a majority of justices do not want to enter this constitutional fray.

There is an interim step. In 1996, Congress passed and President Clinton signed the Defense of Marriage Act, known as "DOMA." It provides that no state shall be required to recognize any same-sex marriage performed in another state, and that the federal government shall not recognize same-sex marriages even if concluded in a state where they are lawful. The Supreme Court could find DOMA to be unconstitutional, as a violation of equal protection and the provisions in the Constitution that require states to give "full faith and credit" to the proceedings of another state.

Were that to occur, much of the heat could be removed from the question, at least for now—individual states would be permitted to decide whether same-sex marriages could be lawfully performed within their borders and, if they could, those marriages would remain valid no matter where the same-sex couple might relocate in the future. This would be hugely important to same-sex couples—they could marry (though, perhaps, not in the state of their choice), and obtain the benefits married couples enjoy in respect to medical insurance, property ownership, estate planning, and a host of other important issues.

In the near term, this is the furthest the Court as presently constituted is likely to go; it allows the Court to address an issue that five justices seem to think is important, but in a way that is far less explosive than a direct ruling on the constitutionality of same-sex marriage.

If, however, President Obama has the opportunity to replace a conservative justice, a more expansive ruling that protects the marital rights of same-sex couples on a constitutional basis could easily result.

There is a possibility that the Supreme Court could be rendered a nonfactor on this issue if Congress passes proposed legislation that would prohibit any form of discrimination against gays. President Obama has sent somewhat contradictory signals on his position: he opposes the Defense of Marriage Act, but during his campaign he said he was opposed to same-sex marriage (but favors civil unions). If this legislation works its way through Congress and is signed into law, it is unlikely that five justices would find a reason to invalidate congressional action of this type.

PRIVACY VERSUS NATIONAL SECURITY. The war on terrorism is necessarily a war of preemption; apprehending terrorists after they strike is important, but because terrorists strike at civilian targets with the intent to inflict massive damage, the focus must be on stopping a terrorist attack *before* it happens. But how do you do that when you don't know who or where the terrorists are? In prior eras, nations would direct espionage efforts at each other's governments and military organizations. Today, such efforts are of limited utility—particularly in an open society like ours, would-be terrorists can live seemingly ordinary lives among us, as they did before 9/11.

So here is the federal government's unenviable dilemma: if it can't know who to watch and investigate, doesn't it have to watch and investigate just about everyone?

This, of course, raises bona fide privacy issues. No one likes to be spied on, and the notion that the government is the one doing the spying is anathema to our concept of a free and democratic society. Benjamin Franklin once said that "they that can give up essential liberty to purchase a little temporary safety deserve neither liberty nor safety." One wonders if Franklin would have felt the same in a world where a terrorist with a dirty bomb or a biological weapon could kill hundreds of thousands of innocent people. In November 2005, 9/11

Commission Vice Chairman Lee Hamilton testified before Congress that the inability of federal agencies to obtain and share information about suspected terrorists "was the single greatest failure of our government in the lead-up to the 9/11 attacks."

Still, unchecked and wide-ranging domestic surveillance, even if well intentioned, can be corrosive to a free society. We act differently if we know we're being watched. One of the key methods totalitarian societies use to dissuade dissent and political participation is the threat of surveillance, the ever-present and implicit "we know who you are and what you're doing."

This is not an irrational fear, and in other contexts the Supreme Court has recognized the issue. The surveillance techniques that are at the government's disposal are monumental and frightening. There are those who argue that if you've done nothing wrong you shouldn't object to government spying, but even those who know they've done nothing wrong value their private lives, and the thought that strangers are delving into your figurative dresser drawers and medicine cabinets is discomforting, to say the least.

Recent technologies, coupled with recent government actions, only heighten these concerns. For instance . . .

We leave electronic trails wherever we go and whatever we do: credit cards, EZ passes, cell phone calls, GPS chips, e-mails, ATM usage, Internet purchases, online searches, postings on Web sites, and so on. Through the Patriot Act and other legislation, Congress has authorized the FBI to utilize "National Security Letters" (known as NSLs) to obtain information of this type, and much more, without prior court approval, based only on the government's statement that it needs the information as part of a terrorism investigation. The FBI has issued tens of thousands of NSLs, and numerous instances of abuse have been revealed.

In December 2005, the *New York Times* revealed that the National Security Administration was intercepting communications between the

United States and overseas locations without prior court approval. In 2006, a *USA Today* investigation revealed that the NSA had installed sophisticated surveillance equipment in AT&T's switching facilities that allowed it to intercept domestic telephone calls and telephone records (such as numbers called and the length of conversations), potentially involving hundreds of billions of calls a year.

Federal legislation requires banks and other financial institutions to report to the government certain financial transactions that *might* be indicative of terrorist activities, but that could just as easily be completely innocent and presumptively private.

In 2002, the Department of Defense unveiled its "TIA" program —originally "Total Information Awareness," later wisely renamed "Terrorism Information Awareness." The program involved, among many other things, a previously unimaginable "data-mining" technology that could search and synthesize any person's transactions (credit card purchases, hotels, rental cars, airplane tickets, and so on), match the data with other databases, and highlight patterns for even deeper investigatory follow-through—all without the person's knowledge.

The problems raised by these kinds of domestic surveillance programs have been played out post–9/11, sometimes contentiously, between the Bush administration and certain members of Congress, both Democrat and Republican, with ample assists from the press and private organizations concerned about privacy rights. This has resulted in changes to certain legislation and regulations, and a variety of new approaches. With the advent of a Democratic Obama administration and a heavily Democratic Congress, further revisions to prior laws and regulations and a panoply of new approaches is inevitable.

What about the Supreme Court's role in all of this? The best guess: in the near term, at least, the Supreme Court is most likely to stay as far away from these issues as it can.

The contours of the privacy-versus-national-security balance are in flux, and we need to get it right: countless lives may be at stake. The ultimate decisions as to how these truly important issues are calibrated will rest largely on the expertise of defense and intelligence experts who have access to classified data. This is what the executive and legislative branches do; it is not what the judiciary does, and the Supreme Court knows that it is not the branch of government best equipped to write these crucial rules. Consequently, both liberal and conservative justices will likely avoid these problems, with the possible exception of extreme and unique abuses, at least until the Obama administration and the new Congress find their footing.

For instance, the ACLU filed a lawsuit challenging President Bush's wireless wiretapping orders—orders issued in seemingly plain violation of an existing federal law, the Foreign Intelligence Surveillance Act of 1978, which mandated that such wiretap orders be approved by a special court. The ACLU did little more than ask that the president be ordered to abide by the law. But as the case was pending, Congress was working on new guidelines. A lower court denied the ACLU request, and the Supreme Court took a pass—it issued a one-line order refusing to accept the case, without explanation. In all likelihood, the Supreme Court thought it best to allow the new guidelines to take shape before it would even consider the legalities.

This should not change all that much even if a liberal majority emerges. In 2007, the Navy began training sailors in the use of certain sonars designed to detect enemy submarines. The exercises were held off the coast of southern California, and there was ample evidence that the sonar blasts were killing and maiming whales and large numbers of other marine species. The case made its way to the Supreme Court, which issued its ruling in late 2008. Chief Justice Roberts wrote the majority opinion, and while recognizing that the concerns for the marine animals was real and serious, he had no trouble deferring to the Navy's judgment on what was required to promote national security. Predictably, his conservative colleagues, who usually defer to the government in the national security arena, joined in that conclusion. But Justice Stevens, one of the Court's most liberal justices, also supported the majority's decision, and Justice Breyer took a cautious middle ground as well. There is no liberal majority with the stomach to dictate national security policy.

There could be exceptions, involving extreme or unusual circumstances, to this hands-off national security approach, such as the *Boume-diene* case that arose out of Guantanamo. A majority saw that case as involving human rights and international law violations implicating constitutional issues that could not be ignored. But other than cases raising such striking issues, the Supreme Court is likely to leave the Executive and Legislative branches to their own devices.

EMPLOYEE RIGHTS. Many liberals in Congress and the judiciary have argued (over the objections of their conservative counterparts) that in the last ten years or so, the Supreme Court has, with some exceptions, given an exceedingly narrow reading to statutes designed to protect employees. During this time, courts all over the country have been besieged with employee versus employer claims, and many liberals contend that the conservative majority on the Supreme Court has reacted to what it sees as an unreasonable burden imposed on businesses.

The reach of the Americans with Disabilities Act, for example, was so limited by Supreme Court decisions that, in 2008, congressional Democrats passed legislation to expand the Supreme Court's narrow interpretation of the original statutory text.

The same thing happened in response to a 2007 decision, *Ledbetter v. Goodyear Tire & Rubber Co.*, which serves as the current poster child for what many liberal thinkers, including President Obama, see as an anti-employee penchant on the current Supreme Court. The case involved a female worker, Lilly Ledbetter, who for many years had been paid less than men performing the same job, but did not know it until she retired. The law prohibiting wage discrimination based on gender requires that a claim be filed within 180 days of the discriminatory act, and on that basis the five Supreme Court conservatives ruled that Mrs. Ledbetter was entitled to nothing—even though, through no fault of her own, she had no realistic way to know that her rights were being violated before the expiration of the deadline. The liberal wing of the Court was adamant in its dissent. Justice Ginsburg read her dissenting opinion from the bench—something a justice does only when extremely upset by the majority's decision. She charged that the majority had chosen hyper-technicalities over justice, and that it did not understand (or chose to ignore) "the realities of the workplace."

President Obama felt so strongly about the *Ledbetter* decision that he invited Mrs. Ledbetter to ride with him on his pre-inaugural "whistle stop" trip from Philadelphia to Washington, and shortly thereafter he signed into law the Lilly Ledbetter Fair Pay Act, effectively reversing the Supreme Court's ruling. He has pointed to *Ledbetter* as the kind of decision his favored Supreme Court nominees would *not* make. He views it as a decision that shows none of the empathy or "heart" he looks for in a prospective justice.

To the extent that the conservative majority makes the Court more business- than employee-friendly, it will stay that way unless and until President Obama has the opportunity to replace one of the conservative justices. President Obama understands that, and rather than waiting for an opportunity to change the Court, he will try to blunt what the Court has done and is likely to do in the future through a pro-employee legislative agenda.

So long as this new legislation is clear, the Supreme Court, be it liberal or conservative, will probably have little to say about it (with the possible exception of constitutional issues raised by the Employee Free Choice Act, which seeks to radically reform the unionization process). The Court's prior decisions, like *Ledbetter*, were not based on a finding that the statutes in question were unconstitutional; rather, they were based on an interpretation of what Congress meant when it enacted the laws at issue. If the language of future laws leaves little to question—and pro-employee legislators will make every effort at crystalline clarity—the Supreme Court's role in the realm of employee rights will be minimized. The Congress, not the Supreme Court, will own the most significant aspects of these issues for the foreseeable future.

CAMPAIGN FINANCE REFORM. In the *Buckley v. Valeo*, Supreme Court upheld regulations on campaign contributions made to candidates running for office. Those who opposed the regulations argued that in today's political process, money is the equivalent of speech—it's what gets you heard—and that restrictions on campaign contributions therefore violated the First Amendment.

Buckley was decided in 1976, and as of President Obama's inauguration, only *one* of the justices who voted to uphold the regulations, Justice Stevens, remained on the Supreme Court.

In *McConnell v. FEC*, decided in 2003, a sharply divided Supreme Court upheld the bulk of BCRA, colloquially known as McCain–Feingold, which regulates "soft money"—contributions made to organizations that electioneer for candidates. Again, opponents argued that regulations of this type violate the First Amendment.

Of the five justices who formed the majority in *McConnell*, two—Justice O'Connor and Justice Souter—have left the bench. Two of the justices who have joined the Court since McConnell was decided—Chief Justice Roberts and Justice Alito—expressed serious reservations about campaign finance reform in the *Davis v. FEC* case, discussed earlier.

So here's what can be said about where matters now stand in the Supreme Court on the soft money issue:

Justices Scalia and Thomas vigorously dissented in *McConnell*— they believe that blanket restrictions on soft money contributions violate the First Amendment. Justice Kennedy wrote a separate dissent in *McConnell*. He concluded that restrictions on campaign contributions are constitutional *only* if geared toward contributions made directly to a candidate or at the candidate's direction (which is not the case with soft money) and *only* if the regulations are tailored to the prevention of corruption. Reading the tea leaves left behind in the *Davis v. FEC* case explained earlier, Chief Justice Roberts and Justice Alito are, at the least, very troubled by the First Amendment and related issues that arise from restrictions on campaign contributions. Justice Alito wrote that while it may be permissible for the government to try to take corruption out of the electoral process, it is "dangerous business" for the government to use election laws to influence the outcome of elections.

When you put all of this together, there may well be a five-justice majority on the current Supreme Court in favor of reversing *McConnell* and its regulation of soft money. There's little doubt about Justices Scalia, Thomas, and Kennedy—they filed dissents in *McConnell*. As for Chief Justice Roberts and Justice Alito, Justice Alito's opinion in *Davis*, joined in by Chief Justice Roberts, seems to augur *McConnell*'s demise. Here's the argument: If, as Justice Alito reasoned, money is what allows us to "robustly" exercise our most revered First Amendment rights in a political contest, how can generalized limits on soft money be sustained? True, Congress can act to limit electoral corruption, but can it simply be *assumed* that large soft money donations lead to corruption? Won't you need proof that the contributions were made for corrupt purposes (as opposed to free speech purposes) before the government can forbid them?

The companion question is whether the current Supreme Court will stop at soft money, or whether it will wash away *all* regulation of campaign contributions, including the regulations applicable to contributions made directly to candidates that were upheld in *Buckley*.

Based on their prior opinions, it is likely that Justices Scalia and Thomas would rule that *all* campaign contributions are protected by the First Amendment except, perhaps, those *proven* to have been made for corrupt purposes (like buying a vote on a particular issue). Chief Justice Roberts and Justice Alito haven't spelled out their overall views of campaign finance reform just yet, but they've left some clear indications in *Davis* that they may well agree with Justices Scalia and Thomas. Justice Kennedy looks, again, like the deciding vote. He *might* not be willing to go quite that far—his dissent in *McConnell* implies that, at least then, he felt that a large contribution made directly to a candidate holds enough potential for corruption as to justify regulation even without direct proof of corruption. But in joining Justice Alito's opinion in *Davis*, Justice Kennedy signed on to some very strident criticisms of campaign finance reform in general, and it may be that he's now in agreement with Justice Scalia and Justice Thomas.

The upshot is that unless President Obama is given the opportunity to replace one or more of the existing conservative justices, the Supreme Court may wipe some, if not all, of the campaign finance reform legislation from the books—and it may do it in a way that will make it impossible, except in cases of proven corruption, to take big money out of politics.

And even a Court with a liberal majority is not certain to save campaign finance reform as we currently know it. The stupendous sums President Obama was able to raise even in the face of current restrictions have both liberals and conservatives reconsidering the entire campaign finance reform issue, from top to bottom.

EDUCATIONAL DIVERSITY AND AFFIRMATIVE ACTION. In the 2003 *Grutter* decision explained in Chapter 4, the Supreme Court ruled in a 5–4 decision authored by Justice O'Connor, that a university applicant's race *can* be considered as part of the admissions process, so long as it was just one factor in an individualized assessment, and so long as the reason for considering race served a compelling social interest, in this case the promotion of educational diversity. The *Grutter* decision had obvious implications beyond the university setting, and in the years following lower courts began to explore whether racial preferences could be utilized in other contexts as well.

By 2007, however, the makeup of the Court had changed—Justice O'Connor, the Court's then-swing vote, and Chief Justice Rehnquist, a conservative justice, had left, and they were replaced by Chief Justice Roberts and Justice Alito—the net result being that two conservatives replaced one conservative and one centrist. Justice Kennedy, now the Court's middleman, had dissented in *Grutter*—while he agreed that race *could* be considered to promote educational diversity in very narrow circumstances, he felt that the university policies at issue in the *Grutter* case went too far in practice, and afforded an applicant's race unjustified primacy.

In 2007, this newly constituted Supreme Court decided the case of *Parents Involved in Community Schools v. Seattle School District No. 1.* The case involved a challenge to school-assignment procedures used by two school districts, one in Seattle, the other in Jefferson County, Kentucky. The case is worth considering in some detail; it includes the harbingers of where the current Court will probably take the question of racial preferences in the future.

In Seattle, the school district used three "tiebreaker" procedures to determine which students would be assigned to popular high schools that were oversubscribed. Two of the tiebreakers were race-neutral, but the third considered a student's race as part of the district's effort to keep the racial compositions of each school similar to the racial composition of the district itself—if the school in question already had a greater percentage of whites than the district, that would count against a white applicant. In Jefferson County, the school district had previously been subject to, and satisfied, a court-ordered desegregation decree. It used race as part of its continuing, voluntary efforts to keep its schools desegregated. Students were classified as either "black" or "other" and schools were not permitted to be less than 15 percent or more than 50 percent black.

The *Parents Involved* case generated an array of somewhat-overlapping opinions by a variety of justices, but some themes emerged. Chief Justice Roberts wrote an opinion to which a majority of the justices subscribed—his conservative colleagues (Scalia, Thomas, and Alito), along with Justice Kennedy. This opinion ruled both the Seattle and Jefferson County plans unconstitutional because in each, a student's race, *by itself*, could be a determinative factor in the school-assignment decision. This, the Chief Justice wrote, would violate the rationale of the *Grutter* decision, which teaches that race can be considered *only* if it comprises one of many factors that is considered during a holistic, individualized assessment of the student.

In addition, Chief Justice Roberts included an additional section in his opinion to which only Justices Scalia, Thomas, and Alito subscribed. The Chief Justice's view was that race may not be considered at *all* except in two narrow, socially important contexts: reversing the results of past discrimination (which did not apply, since Seattle had no history of discrimination and Jefferson County had already achieved its court-ordered desegregation goals); and achieving diversity in higher (i.e., college-level) education (which did not apply, since both districts dealt only in elementary and high school education). What these school districts were *really* doing, Chief Justice Roberts wrote, was implementing some form of preferred racial balance—and that, he concluded, is plainly unconstitutional. "The way to stop discrimination on the basis of race," he wrote, "is to stop discriminating on the basis of race."

The liberal wing—Justices Stevens, Souter, Ginsburg, and Breyer—expressed varying degrees of outrage at the Chief Justice's reasoning. Justice Breyer minced no words, writing that the conservatives' position "distorts precedent, it misapplies the relevant constitutional principles, it announces legal rules that will obstruct efforts by state and local governments to deal effectively with the growing resegregation of public schools, it threatens to substitute for present calm a disruptive round of race-related litigation, and it undermines *Brown*'s promise of integrated primary and secondary education that local communities have sought to make a reality."

Justice Kennedy, while agreeing with the first section of Chief Justice Roberts's opinion, had strong disagreements with the remainder. He wrote that, contrary to the Roberts opinion, the pursuit of diversity in elementary and high school education *is* a constitutionally permissible goal. And he concluded that, contrary to the Roberts opinion, racial segregation remains a reality in many schools, and race *must*, therefore, be considered as part of the effort to address that issue. To the extent the Roberts opinion "suggests the Constitution mandates that state and local school authorities must accept the status quo of racial isolation in schools," he wrote, "it is, in my view, profoundly mistaken."

At the same time, Justice Kennedy criticized the liberal wing. The school district policies they endorsed, he wrote, "would result in the broad acceptance of governmental racial classifications." He advocated the use of "race-conscious," but not race-based, means of bringing students of different backgrounds together, like strategic school-site selection, recruiting programs, and other methods that "do not lead to different treatment based on a classification that tells each student he or she is to be defined by race."

As is currently the situation with so many issues, Justice Kennedy's view seems to command a fragile majority. He and the liberal justices on the Court agree that in the educational system generally, the pursuit of racial diversity can be a compelling social interest. But their agreement stops approximately there. Justice Kennedy would plainly vote with his conservative colleagues in outlawing systems that use race by itself as a determinative factor—such as systems that seek to achieve certain percentages of certain races. He will insist that if race is considered at all, it be considered only as one factor among many other important factors that characterize an applicant. And to the extent they are available, he will plainly favor other means to achieve diversity that do not involve the direct consideration of race.

Unless President Obama has the opportunity to shift the current division of views through the replacement of a conservative justice with a liberal justice, this will remain the general view of the Court for the foreseeable future in the educational context. The next question is, of course, what all of this means in other contexts.

The current majority appears very reluctant to permit racial preferences in almost any setting aside from education. It *might* allow some form of racial preferences to be used if there is real proof that they are needed to address substantial operational concerns in an area involving undeniably important social functions. For instance, a police department might be able to prove that effective crime prevention requires a certain percentage of minority officers in order to instill public confidence in the unbiased nature of the police force. Or a prison facility might be able to prove that in order to be effective, it needs a certain percentage of minority correctional officers to quell racial tensions in the prison population. Still, even in these situations, race could only be used as *one* of a variety of factors in the hiring process—hiring a certain number of minority applicants based mainly on their minority status in order to raise the percentage of minorities in the workforce will not be permitted.

These positions create real doubts regarding the prospective lifespan of affirmative action and similar programs. In the face of the expressed views of the conservative majority, do government mandates that require mechanical "set-asides" for minorities still satisfy constitutional requirements? What about the race-based voluntary affirmative action and diversity programs many companies have implemented in the effort to bring more minorities into their workforce? Based on these recent cases, white candidates may have a credible argument that racial preferences of this type are now unconstitutional.

The ability of President Obama to replace a current conservative justice with a more liberal justice might change this result, but it might not. While the liberal justices currently on the Court seem less likely to invalidate racial preferences than the conservative majority, when it comes to race, the usual conservative-liberal labels often have little meaning. President Obama himself has often commented that he sees no reason why his daughters, raised in privilege, should be afforded affirmative action advantages merely because of their race.

The prognosis for racial preferences is at best uncertain: outside of certain limited school diversity programs, a majority of the Supreme Court seems to be in favor of eliminating or, at least, severely restricting and redefining public and private sector affirmative action and diversity programs that are designed to favor individuals because of their minority status. President Obama's Supreme Court appointments may change that dynamic somewhat, but because his judicial selection criteria does not reliably foretell how, exactly, a future justice may view this issue, and because President Obama's own predilections are not all that apparent, this will be a focal point for Court-watchers in the future.

GUN CONTROL. The *Heller* case, discussed in Chapter 6, found that individuals have a constitutional right to possess a gun. The vote in the case was 5–4, along the Court's classic conservative–liberal lines.

What remains to be determined is the extent to which the current Court will allow cities, states, and the federal government to restrict that right in the future.

We know that the existing conservative majority will not allow regulations that amount to a ban on guns, no matter what. In *Heller*, the liberal minority argued that the right to own a gun in a particular locale should be balanced against the public safety concerns that exist in that locale—if there were, for instance, a compelling need to ban firearms in a city that was awash in gun-related crimes, the right to bear arms should yield. The conservative majority disagreed, contending that a constitutional right cannot be so easily diluted. Some basic and obvious regulation would be permitted—keeping guns out of the hands of felons and the mentally ill, requiring guns to be licensed, keeping guns away from schools, and so on—but beyond that, just as in the case of free speech, public policy concerns had to yield to constitutional mandates.

Beyond that, it is difficult to predict what manner of gun control regulations the current conservative majority will and will not permit. The *Heller* case was the first time the Supreme Court had confronted the gun rights issue in almost seventy years. The current justices do not, therefore, have clear track records regarding their views on gun control.

For instance, we simply do not know who among the five conservatives who refuse to permit a ban on gun ownership would similarly refuse to permit a ban on the right to carry a concealed weapon, or on semiautomatic weapons, or on high-capacity magazines such as those used in the Virginia Tech massacre, or on armor-piercing ammunition. Many respected political conservatives hold that *only* the most limited restrictions on gun ownership would pass constitutional muster. In the *Heller* case, the Bush administration filed a "friend of the court" brief advocating a more careful and expansive look at what kinds of restrictions should be imposed on the right to bear arms. But a majority of the members of Congress (not including then-Senator Obama) signed on to a contrary "friend of court" brief advocating that only *very* minimal restrictions would be valid—and Vice President Cheney, breaking with the Bush administration's official position, signed on to this brief in his capacity as "President of the Senate." It is reasonable to assume that one or more of the Court's current conservative majority subscribe to this view as well. Given the plethora of lawsuits that have already been filed for the purpose of fleshing out the permissible constitutional boundaries of gun control legislation, we might know more about where these justices stand in the very near future.

On the other side of the ideological divide, it seems likely that a President Obama appointment would trend toward the view expressed by the current liberals on the Court (though in the Sotomayor case, little is known about her gun control stance). President Obama has expressed his support for a variety of gun control measures that most conservatives oppose, often vehemently—he supports national legislation banning the carrying of a concealed weapon, he was one of thirty-one senators who voted against a bill that shielded gun manufacturers and distributors from liability arising from the misuse of their products, and he voted in favor of legislation that would ban certain kinds of ammunition that can pierce armor, but are also in common use by hunters.

So, looking toward the future, we can safely say that if President Obama only has the opportunity to replace one or more of the liberal justices on the Court, a five-justice conservative majority will remain in place, it will refuse to allow a ban on gun ownership, and while it will probably validate the most rudimentary forms of gun control, it would be sheer speculation to predict what other kinds of regulation the conservative justices might favor.

If, however, President Obama has the opportunity to replace even one of the conservative justices, something very different might happen: a five-justice majority could emerge that views with disdain the newly born constitutional right to own a gun. That new majority would favor broad-based gun control regulations, including an outright firearms ban if justified by ostensible public safety concerns. Should that occur, the importance of the *Heller* decision could be minimized in short order — the Second Amendment right to bear arms could turn into a very limited right, one that is effectively subject to elimination if local officials can rationally justify a compelling interest to do so.

Given the passion attached to the gun rights issue, and the effect that even a one-justice change in the Court could produce, it is very likely that the question of where future Supreme Court candidates stand on this issue will be a focus of future Senate confirmation hearings, just as the abortion issue has dominated the senatorial dialogue since the 1970s.

AFTERWORD

Our goal must be to remain the "government of laws, not men" that our Founding Fathers envisioned. But for so long as men have the power to change the laws, achieving that goal will require persistent vigilance.

Democracy American-Style

Here's the way it's supposed to work. Democracy American-style means that government—Congress, the president, or the local town council—can do what they think best concerning the laws they enact and the actions they take. But, all the while, they know that the Supreme Court lurks in the background, reserving the right to sound the alarm if constitutional boundaries are violated. In this way, our system deters and defeats those who would seek to convert our government of laws into a government of men who substitute their own judgments and interests for our fundamental constitutional freedoms and guaranties. The Supreme Court serves as the Constitution's whistle-blower.

Great theory . . . except, as the foregoing chapters have hopefully made plain, the Supreme Court is itself made up of men and women who may seek to substitute their own views for the Constitution's mandates; and, even when acting in the utmost good faith, their actions are colored by their own foibles, backgrounds, and opinions. The Supreme

Court has the power to police the constitutional compliance of the executive and the legislature, but who polices the Supreme Court?

Given the Supreme Court's power, it can be disconcerting to admit, as we must, that Supreme Court justices, like all humans, are fallible. Moreover, even the most supreme of justices, like all humans, see the world through the lens of the events and norms of their times. Many of the Supreme Court cases discussed previously make this all too plain. The Fourteenth Amendment, for instance, assures "equal protection" and, indeed, "Equal Justice Under Law" is literally carved in stone over the entrance to the Supreme Court itself. Yet for decades, highly respected Supreme Court justices consistently deemed "separate but equal" racial segregation constitutionally acceptable. That precept was ultimately reversed, but it was not reversed because the words in the Constitution changed. It was reversed because different justices raised in a different era and informed by different social values knew it to be wrong—but it took fifty years to happen.

How can a country, let alone a judicial system, function when that which the highest court in the land finds to be a constitutional certainty on one day becomes a constitutional anachronism on the next?

"The Worst Form of Government . . ."

Yet when the array of checks, balances, and interrelationships is dispassionately analyzed, the most remarkable part is this: despite its undeniable failures and foibles, our system works better than the Constitution's framers could have hoped.

The reason for this success lies not just in the design of the system; it also lies in the qualifications and integrity of the people who have served within the system. The axiomatic lesson to be drawn from that reality must never be ignored or forgotten.

The vast majority of those selected to serve on the Supreme Court have been men and women of utmost good faith and open mind who, despite their differences in judicial and political philosophies and life views, treated the Constitution with awestruck reverence. In addition, the Court has produced a pantheon of social and judicial thinkers of extraordinary wisdom—Holmes, Cardozo, Brandeis, Frankfurter, and many more—who perceived the system's weaknesses and pitfalls, and skillfully navigated the country around and through them. The inherent fluidity of the law has only rarely been used to promote personal agendas, and has instead served as a self-correcting mechanism that allows the law to adjust over time to emerging realities.

The result has been the creation of an astounding body of law that has both reflected, and directed, the changing social and cultural landscape of our country. Justice Oliver Wendell Holmes Jr. put it best. "The life of the law," he said, "has not been logic; it has been experience." The way in which the Supreme Court has utilized the experiences of the country, and itself, to channel the law and, in turn, the way we live and function is astonishing.

Clearly, there is room for substantial disagreement over the wisdom of many Supreme Court decisions. It has often taken much too long for injustices to be remedied. In hindsight it is plain that serious, sometimes damaging, errors have been made. But when the whole of the Supreme Court's two centuries of work is reviewed and assessed, it is difficult not to be enthralled. It has become a cliché to remark, as did Winston Churchill, that "democracy is the worst form of government except for all those others that have been tried." In this country, the Supreme Court can take much pride in the cliché's continuing life as a demonstrable truth.

Inventing the Future

In the coming years, the Supreme Court will face daunting issues that have as much to do with philosophy, ethics, politics, and economics as with legal interpretations. Depending on how activist an approach the Supreme Court chooses to undertake, it can literally redefine the workings of government, the electoral process, the war on terrorism, the responsibilities of business, the place of religion, the nature of the family, the approach to climate change, and a host of other issues that will determine how Americans live and work.

The Supreme Court has defined much of our past. We now live in an era in which the Supreme Court is, in fundamental ways, inventing our future.

It has its flaws. It has made mistakes. But, still, no governmental institution is better suited to the task.

RESOURCES

If you would like more information about the Supreme Court, the case histories, and constitutional law, I recommend the following reference material:

Casebooks and Treatises

These books are typically used in university or law school courses. They provide a detailed and scholarly explanation, analysis, and critique of the Supreme Court's most important constitutional decisions:

Barker, Lucius J., Twiley W. Barker, Jr., Michael W. Combs, Kevin L. Lyles, and H. W. Perry Jr. *Civil Liberties and the Constitution.* 8th edition. Englewood Cliffs, NJ: Prentice Hall, 1999.

Cushman, Robert E., and Brian Stuart Koukoutchos. *Cases in Constitutional Law.* 9th edition. Englewood Cliffs, NJ: Prentice Hall, 2000.

Epstein, Lee, and Thomas G. Walker. *Constitutional Law for a Changing America: Institutional Powers and Constraints.* 5th edition. Washington: CQ Press, 2004.

Fisher, Louis. *American Constitutional Law.* 5th edition. Durham, NC: Carolina Academic Press, 2003.

Ivers, Gregg. *American Constitutional Law: Power and Politics.* Boston: Houghton Mifflin, 2001.

O'Brien, David M. *Constitutional Law and Politics.* 5th edition. New York: W.W. Norton & Company, 2002.

Rossum, Ralph A., and G. Alan Tarr. *American Constitutional Law.* 6th edition. Belmont, CA: Wadsworth/Thomson Learning, 2003.

Stone, Geoffrey R., Cass R. Sunstein, and Louis Michael Seidman. *Constitutional Law*. New York: Aspen Publishers, Inc., 2005.

Tribe, Laurence H., *American Constitutional Law*. 3rd edition. Eagan, MN: Foundation Press (Thomson-West), 2000.

General Interest Books

These books are written for non-lawyers interested in the Supreme Court, its body of work, and how the Constitution is (or should be) interpreted.

Amar, Akhil Reed. *America's Constitution: A Biography*. New York: Random House, 2005. A very detailed but extremely readable analysis of the history and meaning of the Constitution's various subjects, ranging from governmental powers to the Bill of Rights.

Breyer, Stephen G. *Active Liberty: Interpreting Our Democratic Constitution*. New York: Knopf, 2005. The views of Justice Breyer, a sitting justice on the Supreme Court, concerning his philosophy of how the Constitution should be interpreted and applied to modern situations and issues.

Greenburg, Jan Crawford. *Supreme Conflict: The Inside Story of the Struggle for Control of the United States Supreme Court*. New York: Penguin, 2007. Inside information from the ABC Supreme Court correspondent gleaned from interviews with justices and insiders.

Hall, Kermit L. *The Oxford Guide to United States Supreme Court Decisions*. New York: Oxford University Press, 2001. A detailed compilation and summary of Supreme Court decisions.

Irons, Peter. *A People's History of the Supreme Court*. New York: Penguin, 2000. An analysis of the Supreme Court's decisions in the context of their times and the political environments in which they were decided.

Rehnquist, William H. *The Supreme Court*. New York: Knopf, 2001. The late chief justice's explanation of the significance and logic of key Supreme Court cases, with insights into the behind-the-scenes politics and influences that often swayed the Court's decisions.

Scalia, Antonin. *A Matter of Interpretation: Federal Courts and the Law.* Princeton, NJ: Princeton University Press, 1998. The views of Justice Scalia, a sitting justice on the Supreme Court, concerning how courts in general, and the Supreme Court in particular, should interpret and apply the Constitution and other laws.

Toobin, Jeffrey. *The Nine: Inside the Secret World of the Supreme Court.* New York: Doubleday, 2007. Inside information from the CNN commentator on how key decisions were made, and the inner workings of the Court.

Tribe, Laurence H. *The Invisible Constitution.* New York: Oxford University Press, 2008. Professor Tribe, perhaps the most influential constitutional scholar of his time, describes what lies behind the words of the Constitution—the historical context and underlying purposes of what was said, and how the varying provisions fit together.

Web Sites

These Web sites provide a wealth of current and historical information and commentary about the Supreme Court. Some offer access to searchable databases which include the Court's opinions, briefs submitted by the litigants, and audiotapes of the oral arguments made in some of the most famous and important Supreme Court cases.

http://www.supremecourtus.gov/: The official Web site of the Supreme Court. Includes information about the Court, pending cases, and recent opinions, as well as other features, such as copies of briefs submitted by the litigants.

http://supct.law.cornell.edu/supct/context.html: Cornell Law School, Legal Information Institute, Supreme Court Collection. An excellent source of information about the Supreme Court, with easy access to current cases, and six hundred of the Court's most important decisions.

http://www.gpoaccess.gov/constitution/browse.html: A service of the U.S. Government Printing Office. Provides an annotated explanation of each provision of the Constitution, with citations and links to important Supreme Court cases.

http://www.oyez.org/oyez/frontpage: Includes not only information on pending and recent Supreme Court decisions, but also hundreds of hours of actual audiotapes from oral arguments presented in famous Supreme Court cases.

http://www.scotusblog.com/wp/: A current report on Supreme Court decisions, including commentary and analysis from a variety of points of view.

http://otd.oyez.org/: An online clearinghouse for news about decisions handed down by the U.S. Supreme Court and the cases accepted for review.

http://news.yahoo.com/i/701: A compilation of Supreme Court news stories and commentaries from a variety of sources.

INDEX

Note: Page numbers in *italics* include illustrations and photographs.

PICTURE CREDITS